who knew?

EVERYDAY
COST-CUTTERS

• •

who knew?

EVERYDAY
COST-CUTTERS

Ingenious Ways to Save
without Sacrificing a Thing

BRUCE LUBIN & JEANNE BOSSOLINA-LUBIN

CASTLE POINT
PUBLISHING

Cover design by Lynne Yeamans
Layout and interior design by Susan Livingston

Castle Point Publishing
58 Ninth Street
Hoboken, NJ 07030
www.castlepointpub.com

ISBN: 978-0-9883264-8-4

Printed and bound in the United States of America

2 4 6 8 10 9 7 5 3

Please visit us online at www.WhoKnewTips.com

Dedication

To Jack, Terrence, and Aidan, as always.

Acknowledgments

Thanks to Jennifer Boudinot, Heather Rodino,
Lindsay Herman, and everyone on
team Who Knew?! Extra special thanks to
Melissa Grover and Todd Vanek at Bang Printing.

Contents

Introduction

. . . .

Everyone enjoys saving money, especially when it's on bills, gas, groceries, and other daily expenses that seem to eat up paycheck after paycheck. But what not everyone realizes is that it can be easier than you think to save money on these kinds of expenses without sacrificing a thing.

This informative and fun compilation of tips will give you thousands of ways to do just that. Learn the simple secrets that can save you money while shopping online. Drive your car farther for less money with our ways to save on road trips. Make the food in your kitchen last longer with simple storage tips like storing bread with a stalk of celery! Use vinegar, lemon, and other things you have around your home to make inexpensive, non-toxic cleaners. Never buy bug spray again with our all-natural remedies for getting rid of pests! All of this and more will help you save so much, you won't be able to resist sharing with your family and friends.

We hope you enjoy this book of easy ways to save money as much as we enjoying putting it together. If we missed your favorite cost-cutter, please share it with us! You can always find us at Facebook.com/WhoKnewTips and at WhoKnewTips.com.

Thriftily Yours,
Jeanne and Bruce

chapter 1

DIY Cleaning Solutions

· ·

• •

Kitchen Cleaning Tricks

All-Purpose Orange Cleaner Here is a go-to orange cleaner—it works great on all kinds of surfaces such as countertops, sinks, greasy stoves, and more. All you need are the peels of several oranges, plain white vinegar, water, a spray bottle, and a glass jar with screw-top lid (a Mason jar works perfectly). Place the orange peels in the glass jar, cover with vinegar, and leave for several weeks in a cool spot. Then transfer some of the mixture to a spray bottle and add two parts water. Shake to combine, and it's ready to use. Your family will love the scent!

Squeegee Your Marble Clean We love this great tip for cleaning marble countertops: Use a squeegee! Using the spongy side, you can clean the counters with warm, sudsy water, then remove excess water with the rubber blade. You can also try the squeegee with stainless steel. It's perfect for surfaces that easily get watermarks!

For the Brightest White Cabinets White kitchen cabinets can be beautiful, but they can also show grease, dust, and dirt more than their darker counterparts. To keep them looking their best, add water to a small amount of baking soda until it's a runny paste. Scrub the mixture on the cabinets, and then rinse with warm water. If your cabinets are streaky from commercial cleaners, remove the buildup with a solution of half water, half white vinegar.

Who Knew? Reader's Tip

If your child happens to get permanent marker on the kitchen cabinets, you may be able to remove it with toothpaste. Add a little of the paste (the non-gel variety works best) to the spot and scrub until the marker disappears. Wipe the area with a clean, damp cloth and no one will ever know that the permanent marker fell into the wrong hands.

—*Susan Gillette, via Facebook*

Simple Solution for a Sparkling Stove Do the gas burners on your stove need a major makeover? Removing caked-on grime is easy, but it requires calling in the big guns: household ammonia. Pour ¼ cup into a large Ziploc bag, place two burners inside, and seal. Let the fumes work overnight, then rinse and rub with a rag or paper towel. Stovetop perfection!

The Clean Stove Trick Save on household cleaners by keeping your stove neater. How? When cooking, cover un-used burners with a baking sheet or pizza pans. The pans will catch all the splatter, and they're easy to stick in the dishwasher afterward!

Hair-Dryer Trick If you're having trouble cleaning off the baked-on grease and grime on your range's hood or other areas around your stove, make your job easier without the help of harsh commercial cleaners. Instead, warm it up by blasting it with your hair dryer. Once it's warm, it will wipe right off with a damp cloth.

Cease Grease! Forget about buying those expensive stove cleaners to get rid of cooked-on grease stains. Just wet the stains with vinegar and cover with baking soda. After watching the fun, foaming reaction, wipe with a damp sponge and buff with a dry, clean cloth.

Hassle-Free Oven Spill Oops, that pot in your oven boiled over, and there's a sticky mess on the bottom of your oven! To easily clean any oven spill, sprinkle salt on top as soon as possible. After a little while in a hot oven, the spill will turn to ash and you can easily clean it.

Caked-On Food, Go Away! If you're cleaning your oven, make the job a bit easier with this solvent. Blend ¼ cup ammonia with a box of baking soda to make a soft paste.

Apply this mixture to the stained, cooked-on spots inside your oven and let it sit overnight. Rinse well with tap water the next day, and your oven will look good as new.

Who Knew? Reader's Tip

After you've cleaned your oven racks, coat the sides with a bit of vegetable oil. They'll slide in and out of the oven with ease.
—*Claire Beevers, via WhoKnewTips.com*

Not a Fan of Oven Fans? Oven fans are magnets for grease. If your fan filter is removable, the simplest way to clean the resulting mess is to pop out the filter, then run it through your dishwasher on the top shelf. If it's very greasy, run it with pots and pans or by itself.

See Food Clearly To clean the smudged, greasy, food-flecked window of your microwave or toaster oven, use ashes from your fireplace. Rub them onto the window with a wet rag, then rinse clean. You won't believe how well they work!

Moisten a Mess in the Microwave To loosen a caked-on mess in your microwave, cover the area with a wet dishrag, and microwave it for 15–20 seconds. When the cloth is cool enough to touch, just wipe the spill away.

Quick Microwave Cleanup Microwave odors? Cut a lemon in quarters and put it in a bowl of water, then place in the microwave on high for two minutes. Wipe the inside with a soft cloth and any stains will lift easily.

News Flash: Shiny Sink Nothing makes a kitchen look better than a shiny kitchen sink, and luckily, there's a cheap and easy method for getting one: Just use newspaper, which will make your sink even shinier than a rag will. A tougher option is aluminum foil—crumple it up and scour with the shiny side.

Who Knew? Reader's Tip

If there are a bunch of soap suds in your sink that refuse to go away, throw a bit of salt on top of them. The salt will break their bonds and the bubbles will disappear down the drain instantly.
—*Dennis DeChiara, via Facebook*

Keep Your Kitchen Drain Clear To prevent a drain from getting clogged, periodically pour some used coffee grounds into it. The coffee's acids will break up grease and the grounds' rough texture will help dislodge buildup so that the drain runs smoothly. This works even in drains that don't have garbage disposals!

Who Knew? Reader's Tip

One of the best ways to eliminate odors from your refrigerator is to hollow out a grapefruit or orange, fill it with salt, and place in the back of the fridge. Leave it there until the salt gets completely damp, and then throw the whole thing out and replace.

—*Monica Crawford, via Facebook*

Clean Your Coffeemaker For the best-tasting coffee, make sure to clean your coffeemaker regularly. Just add several tablespoons of baking soda to your pot, fill it with water, and run it as usual. Then repeat using only water. You can also use a denture-cleaning tablet instead of baking soda.

Now Clean Your Coffee Grinder! Even your coffee grinder needs a good clean every now and then, and uncooked rice can do the job. Simply mill a handful of rice as you normally do to your coffee beans. The chopped rice cleans out the stuck coffee grounds and oils, and absorbs

KITCHEN SPONGE SECRETS

Microwave Miracle Smelly sponge? Make it as good as new by quickly killing the dangerous bacteria that make their home in it. Wet it and wring it out, then microwave for two minutes. (Don't nuke a dry sponge, or it might ignite!)

Easy Sponge Disinfection To make your kitchen sponges and brushes last longer, wash them once a week in the utensil compartment of your dishwasher with a load of dishes. This will ward off bacteria and mildew before they start!

Easy Steel-Wool Substitute You have a pot that's in need of a good scrubbing, but you're out of steel wool. Simply reach for the aluminum foil! Roll it into a ball and use it to scrub off caked-on grease. This is also a great way to reuse foil before you recycle it.

Conserve Steel-Wool Pads It's easy to keep your soaped steel-wool pads from rusting: Wrap them in aluminum foil and store in your freezer, even when wet! Any ice that forms will quickly melt away when under hot water again.

Sponge Pot Finding the right resting spot for sponges and steel wool can be tough, because any moisture will lead to mildew. An ordinary soap or sponge dish will do, but even better is using the tray to a terra-cotta plant pot. Its porous surface is designed to soak up water, so put it to work!

the stale odors to boot. Afterward, throw away the rice, wipe the grinder clean . . . and brew fresh coffee!

Deodorize the Disposal A quick and easy way to deodorize your in-sink garbage disposal is to grind an orange or lemon peel inside it every so often. It will get rid of grease—and smell wonderful!

Dishes and Dining

Blender Cleaner Wash your blender in less than a minute with this simple trick! Just fill it halfway with hot water, then add a drop of dishwashing liquid, cover with its lid, and hit blend for 30 seconds. Suds will fill your blender and clean it without you having to disassemble the whole contraption.

Club Soda Cookware Cleaner Here's a dishwashing trick that will save you a lot of scrubbing time! After you've finished cooking, add some club soda to empty pots and pans (just enough to cover their bottoms). By the time you're done eating, the bubbles in the soda will have loosened the grime, making your cleaning job much easier.

Rust Remover To treat rust on metal baking dishes and cookware, sprinkle powdered laundry detergent on the spot, then scour with the cut side of half a raw potato. Who knew?

···

Smooth Grating Problem: You want to break your addiction to buying pre-grated cheese in bags, but cleaning up the cheese grater is always a pain. Solution? Put the grater in the freezer or run it under cold water for several minutes before grating, and the cheese won't stick.

Who Knew? Reader's Tip

If you get frustrated when struggling to clean hard-to-reach spots in bottles, jars, pitchers, and vases, try adding this magic ingredient to your dish soap: rice. Yep, just your everyday rice. The grain's abrasive properties act like a scouring pad on dishware. Combine rice, soap, and water in a container, shake it up, and use as you would regular dish soap.   —*Anthony McArthur, via Facebook*

Eliminate Gunk from Pots and Pans Feeling hopeless about the seemingly permanent baked-on gunk on your pots and pans? Don't trash them yet: Hydrogen peroxide will come to the rescue! Mix peroxide with baking soda until the mixture forms a paste. Coat your dirty pan with it, making sure you rub the mucky areas particularly well, and let stand for at least an hour so the grime-fighting powers can work their magic. Soak in warm water and wipe down with a scrub sponge, and the nasty crud will miraculously wash off.

A Way with Aluminum To remove stains from aluminum pots, fill the pot halfway with water and add ¼ cup vinegar or lemon juice. Bring to a boil, and simmer for several minutes before washing as usual. For particularly stubborn stains, try cream of tartar. Sprinkle a few teaspoons cream of tartar on the stain, and add a cup or two of water. Bring the mixture to a boil for a few minutes, then wash as usual.

Keep Tomatoes from Staining Your Plastic Plastic containers are perfect for keeping leftovers and sauces, but tomato sauce will often stain clear plastic. To keep this from happening, simply spray the container with non-stick cooking spray before pouring in tomato-based sauces. To remove a plastic stain, cover the area with mustard and leave overnight.

Camouflage a Crack in Your China Antique dealers use this trick to hide hairline cracks on china plates and cups. Simmer the piece in milk for 45 minutes. Casein, a milk protein, may fill in the crack, depending on its size. If your china is old or fragile, though, this could backfire—heat can cause pieces to expand and crack.

....

Nix the Nicks Buff away a nick on the rim of a glass or your china with the fine side of an emery board. Don't use a metal nail file or sandpaper; both are too coarse and will scratch the glass.

Who Knew? Reader's Tip

There's no need to buy expensive dishwashing liquid. Buy the cheapest brand you can find, then add a few tablespoons of white vinegar to the water while you're washing, and your dishes will shine. The same is true for dishwashers: Vinegar will remove spots from glass in a flash.

—*Allie Turner, via Facebook*

Easy Egg Cleanup Do you often make eggs for breakfast? Then this tip could change your life! Cold water cleans egg off pans and utensils much better than hot water. Hot water tends to cause the protein to bind to surfaces and harden. Use cold water when washing your egg pans, and they'll get clean much more quickly and easily.

....

Bungled Beaters If your hand mixer isn't what it used to be thanks to jiggling beaters, hardened food in its sockets may be to blame. Take out the beaters and clean out the sockets with a toothpick or bobby pin.

Who Knew? Reader's Tip

There's nothing like a gooey, smelly basting brush to ruin your mood. Put a stop to it today! After your usual washing routine with hot water and soap, dry it off a bit by shaking. Then pour some salt into a cup and place the brush inside. Any remaining wetness will be absorbed by the salt, leaving the bristles as clean as can be!
—*Cathi Steinert, via WhoKnewTips.com*

Get Rid of Food Smells If your plastic storage containers smell like garlic, onions, or another potent food, wash them thoroughly, then stuff crumpled newspaper inside before snapping on the lids. In a few days, the odor will be gone.

Soap Savvy You know you're not supposed to use "regular" dishwashing liquid in your dishwasher, but . . . what do you do when you're out of powdered detergent and company is on its way? The truth is, you *can* use some of the liquid kind—just use only a few drops, and fill the rest of the detergent container with baking soda. It will stop the soap from producing too many suds.

Who Knew? Reader's Tip

Step up your dishwasher's game with a little bacteria-fighting hydrogen peroxide. Combine 2 ounces peroxide with your usual detergent—not only will it kill germs, but your dishes and glasses will sparkle like never before!

—*Jorie Roberson, via Facebook*

Supercharge Your Detergent To boost the power of your dishwasher detergent, sprinkle a little baking soda in the dishwasher every time you run it. It will also help fight foul odors before they start.

Easy Bathroom Cleaning

Spick-and-Span Shower Doors Need to clean those dirty glass shower doors? You can wipe them down with leftover white wine (if you haven't finished it off!). The wine contains the perfect amount of alcohol to battle soap scum and lime. Apply with a damp sponge, leave for five minutes, then rinse off. Finish by quickly buffing with a clean, dry cloth.

....

Fabric Softener Sheets to the Rescue To clean chrome-plated fixtures in your bathroom instantly, always keep fabric softener sheets handy. Just wipe, and the chrome will sparkle. Rubbing alcohol also does the trick.

....

Perfect Porcelain Steel wool and scouring powders will scratch porcelain, so if your sink or tub is made of this fragile material, rub a freshly cut lemon around the surface to cut through grease, then rinse with running water.

Who Knew? Reader's Tip

After a shower or bath, hang your bath mat to air-dry with a pants hanger! Just clip the mat onto the hanger, and hang on the shower-curtain rod.
—*Lexi Jackson James, via Facebook*

Get Rid of That Ring If your shaving cream can is leaving rusty rings on the side of your tub or sink, perform this trick right after you purchase a new container: Coat the rim around the bottom of the can with clear nail polish, then let it dry. The polish will keep out water, so the can won't rust.

....

Rub-a-Dub-Dub No matter how hard we scrub, we never seem to get the corners of our tub clean. Luckily, we have a clever solution! Soak cotton balls in your tub cleaner (or just some rubbing alcohol) and leave one in each corner of your tub overnight. By morning, they'll be as clear as day.

Who Knew? Reader's Tip

Here's a great way to get rid of grout stains in your shower and tub—shaving cream! After the last person of the day has showered, apply shaving foam to the grout, whose stains have already started to loosen thanks to the steamy shower. After that, it's as easy as leaving on until the first shower the next day! Repeat for a day or two and your grout stains will be gone. Best of all, shaving cream doesn't contain bleach so it's less harsh on your grout!   —*Chris Curran, via email*

Do Away with Grout Stains Icky grout stains can really get you down. Grout is porous, so it tends to absorb a yucky mixture of water, dirt, and mold that leaves muddy filth stains on your formerly white tiled surfaces. Spraying and scrubbing weren't doing the job on our kitchen and bathroom tile for the longest time, and then we found this nifty miracle worker: Clorox Bleach Pens. Run a pen over stained grout lines, let set for 20 minutes, then wipe away with a damp cloth. No mess, no stains!

Get Rid of Copper Stains Removing blue-green stains caused by high copper content in your water can be challenging, even with the help of bleach. Try treating your shower or tub with a paste of equal parts cream of tartar and baking soda. Rub into the stains, leave for half an hour, and rinse well with water. Repeat if necessary.

Clogged Showerhead? It's easy to remove mineral deposits from a showerhead without using harsh chemicals. Just unscrew it and submerge in white vinegar overnight, and the clogs will disappear. If you can't unscrew it, fill a small, sturdy bag with vinegar and attach to the showerhead with duct tape, or use an old toothbrush and vinegar. To clean the screen in your showerhead, wash it with water mixed with a dash of dishwashing liquid.

Power Shower Spray Stay on top of mold and mildew by keeping this daily shower spray within easy reach of all family members. Mix one part vinegar with 10 parts water in an empty spray bottle and you're ready to go. Bonus:

You don't have to worry about a toxic cleaner hitting the baby's bath toys.

Scouring Powder Substitute The best thing about scouring powder is its abrasive action. The worst is the harsh chemical smell. To get all the benefits without the caustic chemicals, use baking soda instead. In most instances, baking soda will work just as well as scouring powder.

Who Knew? Reader's Tip

Here's an all-natural way to clean your mirror that will also give it a spotless shine: Wipe the mirror with a clean cloth dipped in strong, cool tea. Buff with a dry cloth and you're done!

—*Manikka Stringer, via Facebook*

Say Good-bye to Soap Scum Keep soap scum off the walls of your shower with this easy trick: Just rub wood furniture polish onto the tile and doors after you clean them, and soap scum and mildew won't stick.

New Life for an Old Loofah If you use a loofah bath puff in the shower, you know that it eventually loses its shape. When your loofah's life in the shower is over, reuse it around the house to clean countertops, sinks, and tubs. It won't scratch delicate surfaces, while still helping to scrape off dirt!

Plop Plop, Fizz Fizz Who loves cleaning the toilet? Not us, and probably not you either. To make this nasty chore easier on your gag reflex, drop two Alka Seltzer tablets into the bowl twice a week. After 15 minutes, swipe around the bowl with a toilet brush. Your toilet will be spotless and fresh as new!

Who Knew? Reader's Tip

Need to remove mildew from a plastic shower curtain? Try running it through the washing machine with two large, white bath towels. Add a little bleach in with your usual detergent, and use 1 cup white vinegar in the rinse cycle to prevent future mildew growth.

—Jessica Dekker Cullen, via Facebook

Ceramic Clean-Up The easiest way to clean ceramic tile is with rubbing alcohol. Just pour it straight on, and mop or wipe until it dries.

Safe Septic Tank Cleaner When buying your first new home, you probably thought about the backyard parties and a basement rec room. Cleaning the septic tank? Not so much. Still, the time will come when you will need to do it. Add 2 teaspoons baker's yeast and 2 cups brown sugar to 4 cups warm water. Flush the mix and let sit overnight.

Cleaning Floors and Walls Easily

Tough on Scuffs The easiest way to remove black scuff marks from a vinyl floor? Just use a pencil eraser to wipe the scuff away. It's that easy!

Swiffer Savings Just because you have a wet/dry mop like a Swiffer doesn't mean you have to spend a cent on those pricey replacement cloths! Instead, use a large sock from your "missing mates" pile and stretch it around the head of the mop. It will work just as well, and you can throw it in the washing machine when you're done!

Super Sweeping Super-power your broom by covering its bristles with pantyhose. Cut an old pair off at the knee and stretch the toe over the bottom of the broom, then pull up over the bristles and tie at the top. The pulled-taut mesh will catch even the finest dust and dirt, keeping big dust bunnies from gathering in the bristles of your broom.

Who Knew? Reader's Tip

There are all kinds of new products available to get your floor clean, but sometimes a simple straw broom is your best bet. Soak the broom's bristles in a bucket of warm salt water for a half an hour and then let dry. This will prolong your broom's life.
—*Crystal Garito, via email*

DIY Wood Cleaner Wood floors look beautiful and elegant in any home. However, wood has one bitter and persistent enemy: dust, which accumulates quickly and is also very noticeable to the eye. For this reason, wood surfaces require regular cleaning to keep the wood looking smooth and shiny. As anyone with wood flooring knows, store-bought polishes and treated dusters are not only pricey, they also contain strong-smelling chemicals that can linger in your home for weeks. Luckily, there's an easy, safe alternative to the commercial stuff that cleans just as well (if not better!) and smells much fresher. Combine 2 cups hot water with ¼ cup lemon oil. Soak cheesecloth squares in the solution, then remove the cloths, ring out the liquid, and leave to dry. Polish wood weekly or when-ever you notice a sneaky new layer of dust.

Easy Fix for a Scratched Floor If you've scratched your floor while doing some home repairs, it's time to ask your kid for help. No, really! Go to his box of a million different-colored crayons, and pick the one that most closely matches the color of your floor. Cut off half the crayon and place it in an old take-out container (or some-thing else you won't mind getting crayon all over). Melt the crayon in the microwave, then spread the hot wax into the crack. Wax your floor and it will look like new.

The Cleanest Carpet For a cleaner, brighter carpet, sprinkle on a small amount of salt before you vacuum. The salt provides a mild abrasive cleaning action that will clean the carpet without hurting the fibers.

Quick Carpet Cleanser If you have guests coming over and need to clean your dirty carpet fast, mix a cup of am-monia with a quart of water. Use a mop to rub this solu-tion onto the carpet, and it'll help remove the grime. You might want to test this method beforehand on an unseen area, such as underneath a chair. Do not use this mixture on wool carpets.

CARPET STAIN SOLUTIONS

Clean Grease Like Lightning Grease can be hard to remove from carpet. Our trick? Cornstarch. Pour a large amount of cornstarch on top of the spot and gently stir it with your finger. Let it sit for a day, then use your vacuum cleaner to suck away the cornstarch. If necessary, add more cornstarch and repeat the process until the stain completely disappears.

Coffee-Stained Carpet Beat carpet coffee stains with egg yolk? You bet! Rub a beaten egg yolk into the coffee stain, leave for five minutes, then rinse with warm water.

Best Gum Remover The best way to get gum out of carpet (or clothes, or hair) is with a chemical called methyl salicylate, which you can find in analgesic heat rubs, like Bengay. Put it on the gum, then apply heat with your hair dryer set on low. Press a plastic sandwich bag on the gum and it should pull away easily. When it's gone, wash the area.

Muddy Mayhem To get rid of dirt stains, first scrape off any that has dried. Then rub a bit of shampoo into the soiled area and let sit for five minutes. Then rub with a damp cloth, wringing out and rubbing again until the soap is gone.

Ink Answers Got an ink stain out of your carpet? Spray ultra-stiffening hair spray on the spot, then leave for 10 minutes. Dab with a wet cloth until the hair spray and the ink are gone.

Raise Matted Carpet If a piece of furniture has matted down a section of your carpet, you can raise up the nap with a simple trick: Let an ice cube melt into the matted area, then rub with a dry cloth.

Who Knew? Reader's Tip

I love to use the plastic bags that newspapers come in to clean the reusable filter bag in my portable vacuum cleaner. I slip my hand in the plastic bag, grab all the lint, and then invert the bag for a more thorough and dust-free cleaning process.

—*Gayle Holmlund, via email*

A Shocking Solution If you can't escape static electricity on your carpet, here's an easy fix. Mix 3 cups water with ½ cup liquid fabric softener, put it in a spray bottle, and apply to your carpet. Not only will the static electricity disappear, but the mixture will serve as a carpet deodorizer too.

Make Colors Last Brighten faded rugs by rubbing them down with a rag that has been soaked in salt water, then wrung out. Or, submerge the rug in a solution of salt water, then wash as usual.

Cleaning Solutions for Furniture and Other Objects

Prevent Sun Stroke on Wood Furniture Keep your good wood furniture out of direct sunlight as much as possible, especially during the hot summer. It damages the finish and can bleach the wood.

Remove Marks from Wood If you have a white mark on your wooden table and you're not sure where it came from, it may have been caused by putting a hot dish or mug onto the area. Luckily, you can easily remove this spot with a couple of household helpers. Just grab some toothpaste (as long as it's not the whitening kind) and place a dollop of it on the table along with a small amount of baking soda. Gently rub the area for a minute, then wipe clean and repeat until the mark is gone. The tiny particles of baking soda suspended in the toothpaste will rub tiny particles of wood off your table until it looks as good as new!

Make Your Own Spray Bottle If you're anything like us, your cleaning-supply shelves are littered with spray bottles. The next time you need a new one, skip the store-bought kind and make your own using an ordinary plastic water bottle. Just poke a small hole in the hard plastic cap, fill the bottle with your cleaning solution, and twist the cap on securely. To use, turn the bottle upside down and squirt!

Be Your Own Mr. Clean Do you love Mr. Clean Magic Erasers? These costly wonders are made from a material called melamine foam. Melamine foam has been used for decades as an insulator and sound-proofer, which means you can buy large sheets of it for less than the cost of a single box of "magic sponges." Buy some online or at a hardware store, then cut them down to size! They'll cost you less than 30¢ each.

The Easy Way to Remove Labels Many store-bought household items come with pesky price stickers and other labels that are tough to remove cleanly. If you're anything like us, you've scrubbed, scratched, and scraped at the adhesives—to no avail. That's why we love this easy-peasy DIY label remover. Just combine one part vegetable oil with two parts baking soda and stir to form a paste. Using your fingers or a paper towel or cloth, rub the paste onto the label until it starts to come off. The oil helps dissolve the sticky stuff, while the baking soda provides the necessary abrasion to rub it right off.

A Great Future for Your Plastics There aren't many cleaners designed especially for plastics, but it's easy to make your own. Simply mix a quart of water with 3 table-spoons of either lemon juice or white vinegar. Pour it in a spray bottle, and you've got some plastic cleaner.

Who Knew? Reader's Tip

It's hard to get more than a few wearings out of a pair of pantyhose, but luckily there are lots of uses for them once they get runs. Save them to use as a dust rag, or use them to buff silver. I think they polish even better than regular cloth!

—*Alexandra West, via Facebook*

Dusting Your Blinds Is there any chore more annoying than dusting your venetian blinds? Luckily, you don't have to buy blinds cleaner. Instead, use bread crusts. Just hold a piece of crust around each slat, then run it along the length of the blinds. An old paintbrush will also do the trick, or you can use the brush attachment on your vacuum cleaner.

Let Plants Breathe When you're dusting your home, don't forget your plants! Dust buildup can prevent plants from getting needed air, so spray them with water or wipe down the leaves with a cloth. Baby wipes and used fabric softener sheets are also good for wiping down leaves. You can even use the inside of a banana peel!

Who Knew? Reader's Tip

One of the best cleaners for copper is a simple lemon! Cut it in half, sprinkle the cut side with salt, and rub over the surface you're cleaning. Rinse with cold water and watch it shine.

—*Clark Greenman, via Facebook*

Bath Time for Plants! If you're like us, you rarely have the time to dust your houseplants. If they're smaller, here's a way to make quick work of the job: Simply stick your plants in the tub and turn the shower on for a few seconds. Not only will the water get rid of dust buildup, the plants will also get a deep watering.

Cleaning a Crystal Chandelier If you have a crystal chandelier, don't dread cleaning it any longer! First, make sure the light switch is off. Next, lay a blanket or upside-down umbrella underneath the chandelier to catch any drips or falling pieces. Now mix ½ cup rubbing alcohol with 1½ cups water in a jar. The crystals clean them-selves—all you have to do is bring the jar up to each one and dip it in, then let it air-dry. You can use a little bit of the solution on a clean cotton rag to wipe areas that can't be dipped.

Get a Lampshade Dust Free The trick to cleaning a pleated lampshade is finding the right tool. Stroke each pleat from top to bottom with a dry, clean paintbrush. Or use a rolling lint remover for a quicker clean. If you dust your shades with a fabric softener sheet, its static-fighting properties will keep them cleaner for longer.

Who Knew? Reader's Tip

After you've used a piece of cheesecloth, don't toss it. Throw it into a load of laundry, then use it as a dust rag. It will trap small particles in its weave, and won't leave behind a bunch of lint.
—*Fanny Lassiter, via letter*

A DIY Duster for Hard-to-Reach Spots Do you need reach dust trapped between tubes of a radiator or other hard-to-reach places? Wrap a paper towel around the broad end of a kitchen spatula and secure with a rubber band. Spray the paper towel with all-purpose cleaner for extra cleaning power.

chapter 2

Practically Free Pest Control

· ·

DIY Bug Sprays and Remedies

Fly Away Home Keep flies and other insects from flying your way with this body spray. In a small saucepan, bring 1½ cups water to boil. Remove from the heat, and stir in a ¼ cup combination of any of the following dried herbs: spearmint, peppermint, lavender, or lemongrass. Cover, and let steep for several minutes before straining into a spray bottle. Add ¾ cup witch hazel, and shake before each use.

Repel Bugs on the Cheap Don't spend money on bug sprays. Their main ingredient is usually alcohol, so save some money by simply making a mixture of one part rubbing alcohol and four parts water, then spraying it on as you would bug spray. Another natural (and great-smelling) alternative is equal parts water and pure vanilla extract.

Mosquito Magic Our favorite way to keep mosquitoes away? Simply keep a fabric softener sheet in each pocket. A chemical in dryer sheets is similar to citronella, which is used in expensive bug-repelling candles.

Getting Rid of Lice Naturally Nothing strikes fear in the hearts of parents like the words "lice outbreak." The

BUG BITE REMEDIES

A Soapy Solution Ease mosquito and other bug bites by rubbing them with some dry bar soap like Ivory. It will provide quick relief from itching!

Antacids for Itchy Bites Here's a clever use for that roll of antacids you've got at the bottom of your purse: an itch reliever! Crush one tablet with enough water to make a paste and spread it over your bug bite or any other itchy spot.

Tea Trick Tame that painful bug bite with a little tea. Soak a bag of black tea in warm water and then apply it to the bite. The tannic acid will help reduce swelling and pain.

Dressing to Impress We know this one sounds a little goofy, but it actually works. The next time you get a bug bite, try applying a little thousand island dressing to stop the itch.

Vaporize Itchy Bites That jar of VapoRub in your medicine cabinet isn't just good for breaking up chest congestion; you can also use it to stop bug bites from itching. Just dab a little on the spot, and you'll stop scratching in seconds, thanks to the combination of menthol and eucalyptus.

Try a Little Toothpaste For mosquito bites, rub the affected area with some toothpaste. Fluoride works as an antihistamine, and the mint will soothe the itchiness. Both gel and paste varieties will work equally well.

harsh chemicals that are used to fight lice are almost as bad as the lice themselves. Luckily, there is a cheaper, more natural alternative. Cover your child's head (or yours, if the little buggers have gotten you!) with a thick conditioner like Pantene Pro-V. Put on a Disney movie to keep your kid busy, then get a fine-tooth metal comb. Dip the comb into rubbing alcohol and comb through the hair, staying close to the scalp. Between each swipe, wipe the comb on a white paper towel to make sure you're getting the lice. Dip the comb in the alcohol again and keep going. Cover the hair with baking soda, and then repeat the process with the alcohol and the comb. Wash hair thoroughly when finished, and repeat this procedure each day for a week or until the lice are gone.

Removing Ticks You and your dog just enjoyed a fun romp through the forest, but you brought back a souvenir: ticks. To more easily remove them from you or your dog, first wet a Q-tip with rubbing alcohol. Dab it on the tick, and he'll loosen his grip. You should then be able to pull the tick straight off.

Beat Back Bugs with Vicks Spending some time outdoors at a picnic or barbecue? Rub some Vicks VapoRub on your wrists and ankles to repel insects. They hate the smell and will leave you alone!

Keeping Pests Out of Your Yard

●　●

Spicy Solution If your backyard is overrun with bugs, try this spicy solution to keep them away. Dice up 2–3 habanero or other spicy peppers, 2 large onions, and 3 garlic cloves. Add peppers, onions, and garlic cloves to 1 quart of boiling water. Let steep for several hours, then strain into a spray bottle. Before spending some time outside, spray the mixture all over your yard to get rid of all bugs.

A Not-So-Happy Ending for Carpenter Ants Get rid of carpenter ants naturally with this formula: Mix one packet dry yeast with ½ cup molasses and ½ cup sugar, and spread on a piece of cardboard. Leave this sticky trap wherever you see the ants; they will come in droves to the sweet smell. Unfortunately for them, they'll also get stuck. Wait until your molasses mixture is covered with the creepy pests, then throw away.

Picnic Peace To win the war against ants at your picnic, place the picnic table's legs in old coffee cans filled with water. The ants won't be able to climb up the table, and your food will stay safe.

Keep Flies Away from Your Pool There's nothing more irritating than having flies and other bugs swarm around you while you're trying to take a dip in the pool. We've had some luck keeping bugs away by applying a liberal amount of vinegar around the perimeter of the pool with a sponge.

Who Knew? Reader's Tip

If squirrels are making a nuisance of themselves around your home, keep them away with a home-made pepper spray. Take a cup of your favorite hot sauce, add a spoonful of cayenne pepper and a capful of Murphy's Oil Soap, and mix together. Spray the mixture in whatever areas you want the squirrels to steer clear of.

—*Megan Rye, via WhoKnewTips.com*

Deer Repellent If deer are getting to your flower garden, throw a few mothballs on the ground. Deer hate the smell of mothballs. (Who doesn't?) Just be aware that they're toxic to kids and pets!

Keeping Neighborhood Cats Away If your neighbors' cats are causing havoc in your yard, don't even try to go talk to their owners—once the cats are let out there really is nothing they can do to keep them fenced in. Instead, sprinkle the edge of your yard with orange peels and coffee grounds. Cats don't like the smell, and the scraps will eventually create great compost for your lawn.

....

Grandma's Gopher Trick If your yard is infested with gophers (or you've seen *Caddyshack*), you know how hard it can be to get rid of them. Luckily, an old remedy from your grandmother can help: castor oil. Instead of drinking it, pour it into a spray bottle until it's one-third full, then add water until the bottle is full. Shake vigorously to mix, then spray over your lawn and in areas where the gophers hang out. If you find any gopher holes, saturate an old rag with the castor oil and stuff it into the hole. Gophers hate the smell and will stay away.

....

Spray to Keep Possums Away Possums overrunning your garbage cans? Spray the sides with a glass cleaner with ammonia, like Windex, before you put them out on the curb. (Do not wipe or rinse off.) Possums and other critters will stay way.

....

For the (Humming)birds Are ants overrunning your hummingbird feeder? Rub a bit of olive oil at the tip of the feeding tube, and they'll stay away. The ants can't get through the oil, but hummingbirds can.

....

Plants to Keep Mosquitoes Away If you're looking to repel mosquitoes in your backyard, consider adding any of the following easy-to-grow plants to your landscaping: citronella, catnip, marigolds, floss flowers, and horsemint.

Who Knew? Reader's Tip

Mosquitoes are a pain each summer, but you don't have to buy citronella candles, mosquito coils, or the latest gadget—you can just use cardboard egg cartons and coffee trays (the kind you get when you order more than a couple of coffees to-go). Light them on fire, then blow them out and let them smolder in a fire-safe location. The burning smell they produce is pleasant, but keeps mosquitoes away. —*Chantal Landry, via Facebook*

Barbecue Bugs Be Gone! Do mosquitoes hover over the grill when you barbecue? Next time, place a few sprigs of rosemary or sage on top of the coals. They'll repel mosquitoes, leaving your meat in peace.

Ingenious Mosquito Trap Make a mosquito trap with an old 2-liter soda bottle. First, cut off the top of the bottle, about a third of the way down, and put this "cone" aside.

Then add 1 tablespoon yeast, ⅓ cup sugar, and 1½ cups warm water to the bottom of the bottle. Take the cone and insert it upside down in the bottle, removing the cap if it's still attached. Secure with glue or tape. Mosquitoes will be drawn to the carbon dioxide the yeast emits, fly down the cone into the bottle, and be unable to escape.

Keep Bugs Away from Drinks No one likes having to worry about a bee hijacking his soda while having a drink outside. So cover the top of the cup or can with foil, then poke a straw through. Now you can sip in peace!

Plant Savers

Worms in Your Apples? Do you have an apple tree whose apples are infested with worms? These worms are actually caterpillars—the larvae of codling moths. The bad news is that your apples are probably ruined this year, but the good news is that you can easily stop them from coming back next year. To do this, place several pieces of corrugated cardboard all around the base of the tree. When the caterpillars make their trek into the dirt to build their cocoons, they'll choose the cardboard as their perfect home. Simply throw the cardboard away during the winter (or burn it, to make sure you kill the caterpillars) and you'll take care of your problem before it starts.

Easy Earwig Fix Are earwigs overrunning your garden? Here's an easy fix: Bury tin cans (such as tuna or cat food cans) around your garden, about 5–6 feet apart. Bury them shallowly, just deep enough so that their rims are even with the ground. Then fill them halfway with olive oil. Leave overnight, and in the morning you'll find that the earwigs have crawled in and drowned. Empty the cans and repeat the next day! They'll go for the oil instead of your plants.

Who Knew? Reader's Tip

Aphids eating up your plants? Pour ¼ teaspoon eucalyptus oil, ½ teaspoon dishwashing liquid, ½ teaspoon corn oil, and 2 quarts water in a spray bottle and shake well to combine. Spray the mixture on your plants to kill aphids fast.
—*Kelly Budach, via WhoKnewTips.com*

Watch Beetles Bail Plant garlic in your garden to help keep away beetles. Finding some garlic to plant is easy. If a head of garlic you have in your kitchen sprouts, simply plant it with the green part above ground.

Cause a Stink If stinkbugs have invaded your garden, stomping on them can help you in more ways than one. The smell a stinkbug gives off when crushed not only gives them their name but also tells other stinkbugs to stay away due to danger. You should also keep an eye out for clusters of small green eggs on the undersides of leaves. These are stinkbug eggs and should be destroyed by removing them from the plant and immersing them in soapy water.

Who Knew? Reader's Tip

If caterpillars are destroying your trees, the solution can be as easy as keeping them from climbing them. Do this by wrapping the base of the tree in aluminum foil; secure with duct tape. Then wipe petroleum jelly all over the aluminum foil. It might be sort of icky, but imagine how the caterpillars feel! The petroleum jelly will keep them from climbing up the tree's trunk.

—Matt O'Neill, via Facebook

How to Kill Spider Mites Do you have trees that are infested with spider mites? You can make a mixture to get rid of them using ingredients already in your kitchen. Take a pound of flour, five gallons of water, and a cup of buttermilk, mix it all together in a large bucket, and put it in a plastic spray bottle. Use it on your trees once a week, and it should keep the mite population under control.

Clear Out Slugs with Cabbage If you're having problems with slugs eating your flowers and nothing seems to work, your solution might be in the form of distraction. Slugs love cabbage, so planting a few in your garden will ensure they stay away from your flowers and go for the cabbage instead.

Deter Pests in Your Garden If you've ever bitten into a shred of foil that had gotten stuck to a piece of candy, you know how unpleasant the sensation is. Rodents hate the feeling of foil between their teeth too, so placing strips of foil in your garden mulch will help deter rodents and some bugs. If rodents are eating the bark of your tree, you can also wrap the trunk in foil.

Get Rid of Crickets Who knew crickets hate orange peels? Blend together the peels of several oranges with enough water to get your blender moving. Place in the refrigerator for a day, then spread where you often see crickets or around the foundation of your home.

Keeping Pests Out of Your Home

. . . .

Bye-Bye Buggy Plants Keep bugs away from your house-plants with garlic. Place a peeled garlic clove, narrow end up, just under the soil of your houseplant. Creepy crawlers will stay away from your plants!

Who Knew? Reader's Tip

To get rid of gnats, place a banana peel in a bowl, cover the top with plastic wrap, and punch a small hole in it. The gnats will be drawn into the bowl, where they'll be trapped.

—*Marji Williams, via Facebook*

Easy Wasp Killer If bees or moths have found their way into your home, don't panic. Fill a wide-mouthed jar with 1 cup sugar and 1½ cups water. The wasps will be attracted to the sugar and will drown in the water trying to get to it.

. . . .

Having No Pests Never Smelled So Sweet To keep ants, mice, and silverfish at bay, put a few drops of pep-permint oil on cotton balls, and place them wherever you've been noticing the pests. The peppermint smells good to you, but its odor is repellent to these creatures, and they'll find somewhere else to hang out.

Killing Roaches the Green Way Nothing is more revolting than roaches, except perhaps the chemicals we use to kill them. Try using this natural pesticide: Make a mixture of equal parts cornstarch and plaster of Paris, and sprinkle it in the cracks where roaches appear. They'll eat the mixture, and it will expand in their stomachs and they'll die.

Roach Resolution If you've tried every other solution, and those pesky roaches still want to call your house home, it's time to make roach balls. Here's how: Combine 2 cups borax, ½ cup sugar, ½ cup chopped onion, 2 tablespoons cornstarch, and 2 tablespoons water in a bowl, then roll into small balls. Place three balls into an unsealed sandwich bag and place the bags wherever your roach problem exists. Remember, though, that the roach balls are poisonous; be sure to place them where kids and pets can't reach them.

A Good Night's Sleep for Your Pet To ward off fleas from a pet's sleeping area, try sprinkling a few drops of lavender oil in the area. Fleas hate the smell of lavender oil and will find somewhere else to hide. Your pet, meanwhile, can enjoy a good night's sleep—and smell great in the morning.

Mealworm Menace Keep a few sticks of wrapped spearmint chewing gum near any open packages of pasta, and they'll never get infested with mealworms.

Who Knew? Reader's Tip

To help get rid of fleas, try this bright idea. In the room where your pet sleeps, place a lamp without a lampshade, and underneath it a bowl of soapy water. (Be sure to set it far enough away from your pet so that he or she can't knock either over.) The fleas will be attracted to the light and jump toward it, most often landing directly in the bowl of soapy water. Repeat this process every night for a week, or until the fleas are gone.

—*Raymond Pope, via Facebook*

Herbal Help A number of herbs will ward off crawling insects. The most potent are fresh or dried bay leaves, sage, and cloves. Place any of these herbs in locations where a problem exists, and critters like silverfish, centipedes, and crickets will do an about-face and leave the premises.

Kill Ants Dead If you have an ant infestation in your home, here's an inexpensive way to kill them without calling the exterminator. Mix a quarter cup of sugar, 1 teaspoon borax, and 1 cup water in a small container (not one that you eat out of) and pour a bit of the mixture into some bottle caps. Place the caps wherever you see ants. They will carry the poison back to the colony, killing the whole nest. Borax can be found at drugstores. Be careful—this mixture is not safe for pets or kids to ingest.

Stop an Ant Infestation If it seems like ants are taking over your house, try this easy remedy: Sprinkle talcum powder along your baseboards and doorways. It dehydrates their bodies, eventually killing them.

Fruit Fly Fix Fruit flies are always a pain, because they usually hover around fruit baskets and other areas you don't want to spray poisonous bug spray. Instead, spray a little rubbing alcohol on them. They'll fall to the floor and you can scoop them up and throw them away.

Renew Cedar A cedar chest is great for keeping away moths. But if your cedar chest has lost its aroma (along with those moth-repelling powers), restore it with this simple trick: Rub the wood lightly with fine sandpaper.

MOTH REMEDIES

Not Your Mother's Mothballs Mothballs have that telltale old attic smell, and even worse, they contain a carcinogen. Use a spoonful of cloves instead! Store them in little sachets, which you can buy in a craft store, or tie up in old rags. Your closet will smell wonderful and you'll have no more moths!

Soap Sliver Solution When you're storing winter clothes for the season, put a few leftover soap slivers in a vented plastic bag and add it to your closet or chest instead of mothballs. The soap will keep moths from damaging your clothes, and it smells fresh, too.

Cedar Does It Clothes moths are a pain in the neck to get rid of once they've invaded your closets. Since mothballs are toxic, pick up cedar chips at a craft or home store instead. Cedar is an effective, natural solution to fend off those pesky clothes moths—and it smells great. Stick the chips in cheesecloth or an old nylon sock, tie it closed, and store in closets or drawers to keep the pests away.

Get Rid of Moths Have you discovered that some moths got to your winter clothes before you did? If you have moths on an item of clothing, put it in your freezer for two days and then clean as usual. The cold will kill the moths and any eggs they laid.

Repeat every season to make sure your clothes stay moth-free for the entire time they're in storage.

Repel Flying Insects Basil is not just for pesto! If you have a problem with any type of flying insect, keep a basil plant or two around the house. Drying the basil leaves and hanging them in small muslin bags will also repel flying insects—they hate the sweet aroma.

Who Knew? Reader's Tip

If you keep plants in window boxes, paint them white first. The bright, reflective surface will deter insects and reduce the risk of dry rot. It looks great, too!   —*Stephanie Picchetti, via Facebook*

Sorry, Lady(bugs)! Ladybugs sure are cute, but if they're swarming your home they can be unwelcome guests! Use a little lemon to get rid of them. Wipe down walls where you see them with a lemon-scented furniture polish and they'll find somewhere else to hang out. You can also mix lemon essential oil with water instead.

Best Bait for Mice If you've seen a lot of Disney movies, you probably think mice live for cheese. But when you're baiting a mousetrap, a better bet is peanut butter. Since it's sticky, you can be sure the mouse won't grab it and run, and scientists say they love its sweet scent even more than your best piece of Cheddar.

DIY Rat Poison Kill rats while they sleep by poisoning them with boric acid, which you can usually find in drugstores and hardware stores. Mix one part boric acid with two parts peanut butter and shape into pea-size balls. Leave out for the rats to ingest overnight and in a few days your rat problem will (hopefully) be gone. Just be aware that boric acid is poisonous to humans and animals, so don't use this remedy if you have children or pets.

No Mice, For Good If you've got problems with mice getting into places they're not supposed to, fill in any openings or gaps with steel wool. This will kill the mice by causing internal bleeding after they eat it. If you'd rather not kill them, just put some caulk into the crevice, too, which will keep them out altogether.

chapter 3

Savings for Pet Parents

· ·

Saving on Pet Expenses

Cheaper Pet Meds Pet medications are often insanely expensive. Luckily, we've discovered Omaha Vaccine, which offers great deals on meds that cost more elsewhere. Visit OmahaVaccine.com to search for your pets' medications, and get free shipping for orders over $35.

Head Online for Pet Savings Many brands of pet food and supplies have free coupons on their websites. Some we've found include 9 Lives, Alpo, K9 Advantix, Pedigree, Purina, Science Diet, and Whiskas. Jonny Cat, Fresh Step, and Arm & Hammer cat litter all have coupons on their sites as well. And finally, make sure to check out the websites of Petco and PetSmart, which have coupons and information about sales.

Protect Your Pet Is your pet in need of vaccinations that you can't afford? Check out LuvMyPet.com to find a directory of veterinary clinics that offer reduced-price vaccinations around the US. Or check with your local animal shelter to see if they have a program.

Save on Your Pet's Care We all love our pets and will go to any lengths to make sure they are happy and healthy, but this shouldn't mean taking out a second mortgage to pay vet bills. Look at your local shelter to see what services they provide. Many will spay/neuter and administer vaccinations and annual shots for less than half the price of your friendly neighborhood vet.

Who Knew? Reader's Tip

The busiest days at the pet groomer's are Friday, Saturday, Sunday, and Monday. Find a groomer who offers discounts on Tuesdays through Thursdays, or ask your groomer if she will offer you a discount for coming midweek.

—*Patty Blauw, via WhoKnewTips.com*

Value Vet Save on regular checkups at your vet by taking your pet to a veterinary school instead. These vets-in-training are supervised by licensed veterinarians, so you can get good care for much less. Call a vet school in your area to see if they offer clinics for the community. You can find one near you at VeterinarySchools.com/veterinary-school-directory.

Prevent Pet Problems

Stop Pet Static If you end up getting a static shock every time you try to brush your pet, the problem could be the surface you're both standing on. Avoid standing on carpet or a rug; instead opt for hardwood floors, a cotton towel, or outside in the grass. The synthetic materials in carpets and rugs hold static much better.

Who Knew? Reader's Tip

If you accidentally cut your cat's claw too short and it bleeds, fill a small bowl with cinnamon and dip the paw in really quickly. The cinnamon acts as a coagulant and the cat will clench its paw tighter and help stop the bleeding. Then go to the vet.

—*Beth Peters, via Twitter*

Fight Ear Mites If your dog or cat is scratching his ears or shaking his head often, he might have ear mites. To help relieve him of the itch, place a few drops of corn oil into his ear, gently rub it in, then pat clean with cotton or a soft cloth. Use this corn oil treatment once a day for three days. Just make sure to check with your vet first.

CAT BEHAVIOR FIXES

Aluminum Answers To keep your cats from scratching furniture or getting up where they don't belong, cover the area with aluminum foil. They can't stand the feeling of the stuff under their paws.

Sour Puss If your cat likes chewing on electrical cords, we know you need a solution, and fast! Here it is: Unplug the electronics, then rub the cords with a wedge of lemon. Once they've dried, you can plug them back in. Cats hate the taste of lemon and will steer clear.

Cat Scratches Solved It seems like just about all cats think the corner of your box spring is perfect for scratching. If your yelling doesn't convince them that's not true, try putting a fitted sheet made of sateen over it. The silky material won't feel as fun to scratch as the box spring, and your cat will soon find something else to scratch (hopefully his scratching post!).

No More Nibbling If your cat is nibbling on your houseplant—or worse, using its soil as a secondary litter box—here's a tip you need: Simply scatter some coffee grounds on top of the soil. Cats hate the scent and go cause trouble elsewhere! Just be careful: While coffee grounds are, for the most part, good for your plants, too much of them can cause the soil to become too acidic.

Fur-tastic Olive Oil Add up to ¼ teaspoon olive oil to your cat's moist food once a week to stave off hairballs and make his coat extra-shiny.

Prevent Sunburn Did you know that light-colored animals can get sunburn, too? Guard against this by dabbing a bit of SPF 15 sunscreen on your pet's nose and the tips of his ears.

Pet Potty Training Trick One of the most frustrating pet problems to have is your pet relieving himself somewhere he's not supposed to. Leave an open bottle of Vicks VapoRub near the area and the scent will keep him away. Make sure to talk to your vet, too, as sometimes this can be an indication that your pet might be sick.

Pet Feeding Tips and Tricks

Freshen Fido's Breath Wow, does your dog have some strong breath! Freshen up your canine friend's mouth with a parsley tea. Place several tablespoons chopped parsley in a bowl and cover with 1 cup boiling water. Allow it to steep for 10 minutes, then strain into a spray bottle. Spray the brew into your dog's mouth twice every day, and you'll be snuggling again in no time. Parsley contains natural, odor-fighting compounds that help reduce bad breath in dogs (and humans as well!).

Who Knew? Reader's Tip

If you've bought a new brand of food and your dog doesn't want to eat it, put a piece of beef jerky in the bag and reseal it. By the next day, the smell will have worn off on the food, making it seem much more appetizing.   —*Jim Esse, via Facebook*

Never Pay for a Milk-Bone Again When getting a "treat" for being good, most dogs are just excited about a special snack, not that it's in the shape of a bone. The truth is, doggie treats have almost the exact same ingredients as dog food, and most dogs can't tell the difference. Instead of paying extra for dog treats, keep a separate container of dog food where you normally keep the treats, then give your dog a small handful when he's done something reward-worthy.

For Smelly Cats and Dogs Sometimes, your pet is just plain stinky. If you're beginning to notice pet odor when you open your front door, it's time to take action. Add a bit of brewer's yeast (1 teaspoon for cats and small dogs and 1 tablespoon for bigger dogs) to your pet's food, and your pet will secrete fewer of those unpleasant odors.

Who Knew? Reader's Tip

Does your pet have tummy troubles? Give cats and dogs yogurt to help their GI systems. Mix a few spoonfuls with their regular food once a day. Seek a veterinarian's attention if problems persist.
—*Jenna Bays, via WhoKnewTips.com*

Penny Pinching on Pet Food When shopping for pet food, make sure to compare prices at the pet store to those at your grocery store. A recent study found that pet food tends to cost more at stores that are full of people who are already buying pet products!

DIY Pet Products

Secret to Shiny Fur To make your short-haired pet's fur extra-shiny, rub it down with a piece of silk, velvet, or chamois cloth.

To a Cat, Anything (and Everything) Is a Toy Cats love toys, and they aren't picky about where they come from! Don't spend money on expensive cat toys. Instead, use a balled-up piece of paper, a cork, a jingle bell, or anything else they can bat around the house. To make the toy extra-enticing, throw it in a Kleenex box that has the plastic part removed. Cats will love sticking their paws inside to try to fish out the toy.

A Better-Behaved Pooch Many dog trainers say that the key to discouraging bad behavior (like incessant barking) is to startle your dog. An easy way to do this is to fill an old toilet paper tube with uncooked rice or beans, then tape aluminum foil over each end. Shake the tube and the noise will be enough to surprise him out of his bad behavior.

Mutt Munchies If your dog is teething, you can create a cheap chew toy by soaking an old washcloth in water, twisting it into a fun shape, and leaving it in the freezer. Give it to your pup fully frozen, and when it thaws out, simply repeat the process. Be careful doing this with tiny dogs, though, as they can get too cold if they chew on frozen toys too often.

Get Rid of Litter Box Odor If your cat's litter box smells like, well, a litter box, you don't have to buy a new one. Just rinse it out and add a half-inch of white vinegar in the box. Let it stand for half an hour, then swish it around, rinse, and dry the box.

Who Knew? Reader's Tip

Cleaning out your own hairbrush is bad enough, but cleaning out the one that belongs to your furry companion can be a half a day's work. Instead of getting angry next time you snag your pantyhose, give them a second life. Cut strips of hose and lay them over your pet's clean metal brush, poking the pins of the brush through. The next time your cat or dog looks like he just stepped out of a salon after a heavy brushing, all you'll have to do is remove the scraps of hose, throw them out, and replace with new strips.

—*Amy Reichbach, via Facebook*

Easy Dog Toy Dog toys are expensive and can be made from harmful materials. In the Colonial era, kids made their own dolls from rags. A canine version will make Fido just as happy as any designer plush toy. All you need to do is braid together three old dishtowels. Before you start, cut two strips off the sides of two of them. Then use these to tie the tops and bottoms of the braid together.

....

A Fish's Friend If your fish tank is marked with hard-to-remove deposits, just rub the tank with a cloth dipped in vinegar while you're cleaning it, and rinse well. The spots should disappear. Just make sure you rinse the tank thoroughly before putting your fish back in.

....

Easiest Way to Clean a Fish Tank Having fish is fun, but not when you have to periodically replace the water. Make your job easy with the help of some old pantyhose and a wet/dry shop vac. Place two or three layers of pantyhose over the nozzle of the hose and secure it with a rubber band. Remove your fish to a safe location, then stick the hose in the tank and start sucking. The dirty water will find its way into the vacuum, but the rocks won't make it through the nylon.

....

Free Fishy Fertilizer Even old water from your aquarium can be used again! Use it to water your houseplants—they'll love the extra "fertilizer" the fish provided.

....

chapter 4

Ingenious Kid Tips

DIY Kids' Toys

Clever Tips for Arts and Crafts

Creative Solutions to
    Kid-Related Problems

Cutting Down on Kid-Related
    Expenses

Simple Safety Tips

DIY Kids' Toys

To the Beat of Your Child's Drum If you have kids, you know that they often have much more fun with an object that is not specifically a toy—like a cardboard box—than with commercial toy-store options. With just a few items you have around the house, you can make a "drum" that they can either bang on, shake, or scrape for different sounds. You'll need an empty tin can, from which you've removed the label and ensured that there are no sharp edges. Also grab a balloon, rubber bands, dry beans, and some chopsticks. First, fill the can with about ½ cup dry beans. Next, cut off the end of the balloon, so that you can open it up and stretch it taut over the top of the can, sealing it in place with rubber bands. Your child can bang on his new instrument like a drum, shake it like a maraca, or even scrape the sides like a guiro.

Super-Simple Silly Putty This incredibly easy version of Silly Putty requires only three ingredients and takes just a few minutes to make. You'll need ½ cup Elmer's glue, ¼ cup liquid laundry starch, and food coloring. Pour the glue into a bowl, then add the laundry starch. Next, mix together for about 5–10 minutes, until it starts to form a ball. (It may not look like much at first, but keep mixing until a putty-like consistency forms.) Add a few drops of food coloring and knead until the color is evenly distributed. Store in a sealed container in the refrigerator between uses.

· ·

Egg Carton Card Holder If your little ones like to play games with cards, you can help their tiny hands by creating this crafty card holder: Turn an empty egg carton upside down, and cut slits in each rounded cup just wide enough to hold a card. Slip one card through each cup, and they'll stand up straight for easy viewing.

· ·

Tissue-Box Piñatas Need a last-minute party game for the kids? Turn old tissue boxes into super-fun party piñatas! First, use scissors to poke a hole in one corner of a tissue box. Form a loop on one end of a strip of colorful ribbon, then tie a knot to secure the loop. String the ribbon through the corner hole to hang your piñata, making sure the knot stops the ribbon from sliding all the way through. Fill the piñata with candy, then cover the opening and the rest of the box with colorful crepe paper, using glue to secure it. Hang the piñata in a prime position, and let 'em at it!

· ·

Homemade Sewing Cards You may have seen "sewing cards" for toddlers available in toy stores. They help develop fine motor skills, but are basically just big picture cards with holes in them. You can easily make your own at home. One easy way is to start with the front half of a greeting card. Punch holes around all four sides and use a piece of yarn to lace the holes, over and under. Twenty inches of yarn should be more than enough. Put a knot at one end of the yarn. If it doesn't go through easily, use a tiny piece of tape as you would for a frayed shoelace.

Who Knew? Reader's Tip

Here's a free, soft toy for your wee one: an old sock! Stuff it with old pantyhose, fiberfill, or even more old socks, then sew it shut to make a soft ball. Sure, it might not look as impressive as the $10 ones you'd buy at a toy store, but your baby won't know the difference!

—*Puneet Grewal, via Facebook*

Daydream House Tissue boxes can be converted into a makeshift dollhouse. Cut off the tops and place three or four boxes together, cutting doorways between them once you've decided on the layout for your miniature home. Use real doll furniture if you have it, along with pictures of household furniture from magazines, which you can glue to the "walls."

Good Things Fit in Small Containers Use Tic Tac boxes for mini treasure hunts outside. Give one to each child and tell him or her to collect interesting items that will fit inside. Encourage them to think creatively: If a flower won't fit, will a petal? If an acorn is too big, is there something inside the acorn that could be examined separately? When the kids return, have them do a "show and tell" about what they found.

Toy Parachutes Make an old action figure fun again by creating a mini parachute. First, cut out a square from a plastic sandwich bag. Poke a hole in each corner, then thread a foot-long piece of dental floss through the hole, tying a knot at the end so the floss can't be pulled back through. Once you've threaded a piece of floss through each hole, tie their other ends around the arms or—dare we say it—the neck of the figurine. Now you're ready to launch.

DIY Bubbles Warm weather is bubble season for kids who want some outdoor fun. Here's an inexpensive homemade solution for bubble greatness: Mix 1 tablespoon glycerin with 2 tablespoons powdered laundry detergent in 1 cup warm water. (Glycerin, often called "vegetable glycerin," can be found online and at many health-food and vitamin shops.) Any unpainted piece of metal wire (like a hanger)

DIY BATH TOYS

Save Your Bottles Thoroughly wash old plastic ketchup and salad dressing bottles and let the kids use them to play in the bathtub. They're also a great way to wash shampoo out of hair at bath time!

Easy Bath Entertainment For more fun at bath time, take all those little plastic toys your kids have gotten from vending machines and goody bags, and place one or two in each hole of a muffin tin. Then fill the tin with water and freeze. When it's time for a bath, pop one out and throw it in the tub. Your toddler will love watching it melt in their hands and then having a toy to play with.

Get Creative with Craft Foam Colorful craft foam will stick to flat surfaces like tile when damp. To make quick and easy bathtime play pieces, simply cut the foam into various shapes and sizes and they're ready to go. Your kids can affix the shapes to the shower wall simply by getting them wet.

Homemade Bath Crayons Does your child love bath crayons? Make your own with white soap (like Ivory brand) and food coloring! In a microwave-safe container grate the soap with a cheese grater until you have about a quarter cup. Add 5–7 drops of food coloring and a few drops of water. Mix thoroughly, then microwave until warm, about 20 seconds. Shape into a crayon, or push into an ice cube tray for rectangles. Let harden overnight before letting your kids have at them!

can be turned into a bubble wand: Just shape one end of the wire into a circle. Blowing into the mixture with a straw will make smaller bubbles float into the air. For colored bubbles, add food coloring.

Clever Tips for Arts and Crafts

Painting with Peanuts Here's a creative way to use up some of those Styrofoam packing peanuts: as little paintbrushes for the kids' craft time! Poke a plastic fork into each peanut, creating one for every color. The kids can dip the foam in paint and make all kinds of fun patterns. Plus, cleanup is a breeze; just toss the foam-and-fork brushes in the trash when they're done.

Craft Master If you feel like you're all thumbs when trying to glue sequins or small beads to a card or decoration, try using toothpicks for detailed work.

Rolling in Dough Don't spend money on store-bought Play-Doh; make your own at home instead with the following ingredients: 2 cups flour, 2 cups water, 1 cup salt, 2 tablespoons vegetable oil, 1 tablespoon cream of tartar, and the food coloring of your choice. Combine the ingredients in a large saucepan and stir continuously over medium heat until a solid ball forms. Remove it from the heat, knead it until all the lumps are out, and you should end up with a finished product nearly identical to the real thing. Make sure to store it in a completely airtight container; you might even want to dab a few drops of water on the underside of the lid before sealing it.

Who Knew? Reader's Tip

When it's finally time to replace your shower curtain liner, keep the old one and use it for a drop cloth while painting or doing art projects.
—*Kristen Lorfink-Chapman, via Facebook*

DIY Finger Paints for Little Da Vincis Keep your kids busy and encourage their creativity with homemade finger paints: Start by mixing 2 cups cold water with ¼ cup cornstarch, then boil until the liquid is as thick as, um, finger paints. Pour into small containers, swirl in some food coloring, and watch them create their masterpieces (just keep those colorful fingers away from walls!).

Interesting Art Project Get creative with watercolors and candles—but perhaps not in the way you think. Give your child a white tapered candle and have her "draw" a picture on a piece of paper. She won't be able to see the drawing, of course, until she adds a little watercolor paint to the paper—and the picture comes to life. This is an especially good activity for two kids. Let them write "secret messages" to each other, then exchange the papers, apply some watercolors, and see what happens.

Extend-a-Crayon Once crayons break, they can be hard for little fingers to grasp and use. To help make them last longer, slide broken or worn-down pieces into a plastic straw, leaving the tip exposed. The straw will make the crayon easier to hold onto, and your kids will have all of their favorite colors back.

Repair for Pencil Erasers To spiff up dried or stained pencil erasers, gently rub an emery board over the damaged spots. The abrasive surface of the board will file away the unusable top layer on the eraser, and it'll be good as new!

Makeshift Paint Applicators We love painting projects! And who doesn't? They're loads of fun for adults and kids alike. But unfortunately, they can be messy. For less mess and more fun, try this clever trick: Purchase replacement bottles of craft paint and simply swap the tops for screw-on glue applicator tips, like the tip of an Elmer's glue bottle. You'll be able to apply your paint cleanly, and then screw the tip closed when you're finished.

Creative Solutions to Kid-Related Problems

New Diaper Soak When you purchase new cloth diapers, make sure to wash them 8–10 times before using. This will not only increase their absorbency by puffing the fabric up a bit, but it will also make sure all the chemicals used in their production and packaging have been washed out.

Diapers Love Vinegar If you use cloth diapers, soak them before you wash them in a mixture of 1 cup white vinegar for every 9 quarts water. It will balance out the pH, neutralizing urine and keeping the diapers from staining. Vinegar is also said to help prevent diaper rash.

DIY Diaper-Change Mat When you're on the go and baby needs a sudden diaper change, Ziploc bags can come to the rescue! Just rip open a large bag at its seams, lay it on a flat surface, and take care of baby's business.

Freshen Up Your Diaper Pail If you get a nasty whiff every time you open the diaper pail, drop a few charcoal briquettes under the pail's liner. You'll be amazed at what you don't smell.

Who Knew? Reader's Tip

Baking soda is a gift to anyone who is feeding an infant. Keep some on hand, and if (and when) your baby spits up, sprinkle baking soda on the spot to neutralize odors and absorb the spill before it sets.
—*Jennifer Obermeyer, via Facebook*

Tissue Reissue If your potty-trained toddler enjoys pulling toilet paper off the roll, use this trick to keep his TP usage in line: Before putting the roll on the dispenser, squeeze the tube so that it flattens slightly. This will keep the roll from turning too easily, making the amount that comes off the roll manageable.

Keep Lunches Cool No one looks forward to lukewarm packed lunches. Keep your kids' food cold and fresh with homemade ice packs! Pick up sponges from a dollar store, then soak them in water and stick in the freezer overnight. When packing lunch, slip the frosty sponges into Ziploc bags and stash inside lunch boxes along with lunch-meat sandwiches and any other snacks that should be kept cold. The plastic bags will prevent any spills or leaks.

Freshen a Funky Lunch Box Kid's lunch box starting to smell funky? Freshen it up with bread and vinegar! Just moisten a slice of bread with white vinegar and let it sit in the closed lunch box overnight. In the morning, any bad odors should be gone.

Who Knew? Reader's Tip

If your stroller has become unbalanced thanks to the hundreds of shopping bags you have hanging from the handles, use arm and ankle weights that are used for exercise to more evenly distribute the weight. Attach the weights (which come with Velcro) to the bars of the stroller right above its front wheels. Now when your child jumps out, you won't end up with your bags all over the sidewalk.

—*Donna Inklovich, via email*

Makeshift Medicine Dispenser for Babies When baby needs to take her liquid meds orally, try this easy trick: Cut a small hole in the end of a pacifier and stick a medicine dropper inside.

"P" is for Peroxide If you're a parent of young kids, you've probably been faced with a pee stain on a mattress. Try this effective all-purpose cleaning solution to get rid of the stain, odor, and accompanying toxins. First off, soak up any liquid with paper towels until it's fully absorbed. Then, make the cleaner: Combine 1 cup hydrogen peroxide, 3 tablespoons baking soda, and 1 small squeeze of liquid dish soap in a spray bottle. Immediately after mixing, spray the entire solution over the offending spot, and watch the stain vanish over the next 10 minutes. When dry, there might be some leftover baking soda on the surface—just swipe with a paper towel or cloth or use a vacuum to clean up.

Numb the "Ick" of Taking Medicine It's often a battle to get a sick child to take medicine he can't stand the taste of. To make things a little easier, have him suck on a Popsicle for a few minutes before taking the medicine. The Popsicle will not only act as an incentive, it will numb his taste buds a bit, making the medicine easier to swallow.

Make Ripping Off Band-Aids Painless Before removing a bandage from your child's skin, douse the area with baby oil. The baby oil will soak into the bandage and make it easy to remove without hurting her.

Take Off Temp Tats There's nothing kids love more than temporary tattoos—until they decide they hate them. To easily remove a temp tat before it rubs off itself, dab some cold cream on the area, then wipe it off with a washcloth.

Who Knew? Reader's Tip

Have a sick kid on your hands? Keep your couch from getting covered in used tissues with this simple trick: Take an empty box of tissues and use a rubber band to attach it to a new box of tissues. That way, you'll have a mini "garbage can" and tissue box all in one!

—*Michelle Doherty, via WhoKnewTips.com*

De-Grease Sticky Playing Cards An oft-used deck of cards can get sticky and grimy from the oils on our hands. De-grease the cards by placing them in a plastic bag with a few blasts of baby powder. Give it a good shake before dealing the first hand.

Mattress Protector If you need to accident-proof your child's mattress, and you don't have a waterproof mattress cover, just lay overlapping sheets of foil on top of your mattress, then cover with a couple of old towels and then the rest of your sheets. Now onto the harder task: coming up with a potty-training strategy!

The Ol' Chewing-Gum-Stuck-in-Hair Conundrum

Before you chop off a chunk of your kid's hair or attempt to shampoo it out, give this old trick for getting gum out of hair a shot. Massage a small amount of smooth peanut butter into the gum-stuck section of the hair. Yep, it really works: The oils in the peanut butter counteract the stickiness of the gum. If you're out of peanut butter, try mayonnaise or salad oil.

Who Knew? Reader's Tip

It's hard to say good-bye to those adorable frog or ducky rain boots when your kids outgrow them or burst a hole through the toe. Turns out you don't have to. Put a small bag filled with rice or beans inside each boot and you've got yourself two cute bookends for your child's library.

—*Cynthia Huster, via Facebook*

Good-bye to Popsicle Drips Keep messy melting Popsicles from getting all over your kids' hands (and the floor) by poking the stick-end of the Popsicle through a coffee filter or cupcake liner before you hand it over. The filter will act like a bowl, catching any drips.

. . . .

A "Handy" Tip If you've got kids who never seem to know when enough is enough, add water to your hand soap. Your hands will get just as clean, but the soap will last longer! You can also buy foaming soap dispensers, which are good for keeping the amount of soap you use to a minimum.

Cutting Down on Kid-Related Expenses

Do It Yourself Organized activities for your kids are great, but the expense of enrolling them can take a toll. Instead of paying for a pricey arts-and-crafts class, for example, simply search online for the necessary information and hold the "class" yourself. In lieu of signing up for swimming lessons, just take your kids to a relative's pool or a public pool. Spending money on beginner-level instruction is often a waste, but if your child shows an aptitude for a certain activity or sport, *then* you can spend money on more advanced lessons. If you have to cut down on activities or sports they're already involved in, ask your children if there are any they don't really like. You might find they're just playing soccer, for instance, because their friends are on the team.

Who Knew? Reader's Tip

Your kid is begging for school supplies with his favorite cartoon character on them, but the plain versions are so much cheaper! Meet him halfway by buying some stickers of the character and letting him decorate the plain supplies. You'll save money and get a craft project out of it!
—*DeAnna Inman, via WhoKnewTips.com*

Swap Out Your Toys When you notice your kids getting bored with a toy (and they always do), don't buy them a new one. Instead, stash the old toy away in a bag or box. Once you have several toys, swap with a friend for toys her kids have gotten sick of. Not only will you save money, you'll avoid the clutter that comes with continually purchasing new playthings for your kids.

Bargain Backpack This school season, consider replacing your kids' flimsy backpacks with a sturdier (and cooler) alternative: military backpacks. These bags are built to last in the battlefields, so they'll certainly stand up throughout the wear and tear of the school year. You can find them in any Army/Navy surplus store.

Extra Storage for a Three-Ring Binder If your kids are like ours, they have all kinds of problems keeping their school supplies organized. You can help remedy this by taking a heavy-duty Ziploc freezer bag, punching holes in it so that it fits in their three-ring school binder, and filling it with pencils, erasers, and other easily misplaced items.

It's Camp Time The best time to sign up your kids for camp is right after camp has ended. Many camps allow you to pay in advance for the next summer and save 5–10 percent. Ask at your camp as you're picking your kids up this year!

Never Buy a Baby Wipe Again If you have a baby, you know that one costly item that's impossible to use less of is baby wipes. When we had babies, we saved hundreds per year by making our own diaper wipes! They are easy to make and can be kept in an old baby wipes container, a plastic storage bin with a lid, or a resealable plastic bag. Here's how to do it: Combine 2 tablespoons each of baby oil and baby shampoo (or baby wash) with 2 cups boiled and cooled water and one or two drops of your favorite essential oil for scent (optional). Remove the cardboard roll from a package of paper towels, then cut the entire roll in half (you can also tear off sheets by hand and stack them in a pile). Put some of the liquid mixture at the bottom of your container, then place the half-roll in the container. Pour the rest of the liquid over your paper towels and voilà—homemade baby wipes! Let the wipes sit for about an hour to absorb all the liquid, and your baby will never know the difference.

Simple Safety Tips

Baby Bath Seat Make your bathtub baby-size by using a laundry basket as a bath seat! Give the basket a thorough cleaning before using, then simply place it in the tub for baby's bath time. The basket will keep floating toys within tiny-arms' reach and also prevent head-bumps against the tub.

Make Your Kid Stand Out If you know you're going to a crowded place, make sure to dress your children in bright colors so you can easily spot them. To make them stick out even more, buy each kid a cheap helium balloon and tie it around their wrists. Kids love balloons, and so will you when you realize you can see them from a mile away at the mall.

Bike Fixer-Upper When bicycle season rolls around, make sure your kids' vehicles of choice are in prime shape for smooth riding. Remember that after months of sitting in the garage, the bike chain will need a proper lube job: You can fix a squeaky chain with a light spritz of cooking spray. Clean up any remaining spray and let your kiddos hop on!

Bike Know-How Before you buy your kid that bike he's been begging for, make sure it's the proper size. When sitting on the seat with hands on the handlebar, your child should be able to place the balls of both feet on the ground. He should also be able to straddle the center bar standing up with an inch or so clearance. Make sure to buy a bike that is adjustable past this point, so you don't have to buy another one when he quickly outgrows it.

Make Your Swing Set Safer You've just bought your kids a new swing set, and you're peering out the window just waiting for one of them to fall off. Fear no more! Place carpet remnants or free carpet samples from a local store underneath the swings. They'll kill the grass underneath, but your kids would have done that anyway.

Who Knew? Reader's Tip

For safety's sake, it's not recommend to use bumpers in a baby's crib anymore. But if you get one as a hand-me-down, you can use it around it the house: Wrap the edges of a coffee table or other pointy surface to protect toddlers.

—*Samantha Maxwell, via Facebook*

Quick Toddler Fix If you're toddler is his using his new walking skills to get into your kitchen garbage, the fix is easy: Just use a sturdy piece of tape (like masking or electrical) to tape the lid shut. Adults and older kids will easily be able to peel it up and reapply it, but your new walker won't.

chapter 5

Saving Money on Vacations and Family Activities

• •

Finding Deals on Hotels, Rentals, and Airfares

Creative Packing Tips

While You're Away . . .

Finding Deals on Hotels, Rentals, and Airfares

Forgo the Foliage The best summer vacation you'll ever take might not be in the summer. As soon as Labor Day goes by, the rates go down drastically on hotels and airfare to most vacation destinations. Some of the most-discounted areas are the Caribbean, Hawaii, California, and anywhere else there's a beach. In a warm climate, it will still be as hot as ever on the sand. But the price will be much less, and you'll get the added benefit of having fewer crowds. Check out a travel site like Kayak.com for good deals to your dream destinations.

Keep Scrolling When searching for travel deals online, make sure to scroll through a few pages of results before making your pick. Many sites have "sponsored results," which means that companies have paid to be featured at the top of search results.

Let's Make a Deal When digging for discounts on rental cars and hotels, always call the hotel or rental company directly for the best deals. If the only phone number you have is a national, toll-free one, look up the local number

TRAVEL WEBSITES

Find the Best Flight Our favorite site for finding flights is Kayak.com. It aggregates information from all airlines, and gives you lots of filtering options to find the perfect flight. Then it connects you with the airline's site directly to book.

Last-Minute Airfares If you're looking for the best listed deals on airfares regardless of their destination, head over to AirfareWatchdog.com, which catalogs the cheapest fares as they are listed on travel and airline sites, and tells you how to find them. If you normally spend a lot of time trying different combinations of travel dates and nearby airports, this site will take a lot of the guesswork out of it for you.

It's Not Over Till It's Over After you buy a plane ticket, visit Yapta.com. Enter your flight details and they'll email you if the price goes down. Even if you have to pay a fee to change your ticket, fares often fluctuate by hundreds of dollars. This is an easy way to make sure you're getting the cheapest price.

Where to Find Cheap Cruises If you're dying to get away on a cruise, check out CruiseDeals.com, which has packages to Alaska, the Bahamas, Hawaii, Mexico, and just about anywhere else you'd want to go on a boat. The company negotiates with some of the world's biggest lines to bring their customers the best rates on cruises. If you want to hit the water, this is the best place to start.

for that particular location and speak to them directly instead. The closer you get to your travel date, the better—in fact, don't be afraid to call the day before to confirm your reservation and ask for a better rate.

Who Knew? Reader's Tip

Do you have reward points accumulating on several different airlines? Check out Points.com, which lets you keep track of your airline miles and other rewards points, all in one place. Better yet, you can swap points from one rewards program to another! That means if you have just a few points on American Airlines' rewards program, but are close to getting a free ticket on Delta, you can trade in your AA points for Delta points! In addition to all the major US airlines, Amtrak and some hotels participate as well.   —*Joel Tuggle, via Facebook*

The Cheapest Days to Fly Flight days flexible? Try searching for trips that begin and end on a Tuesday or Wednesday, when we've found that flights throughout the US and Canada are cheaper.

Rental Car Discounts Looking for online coupon codes for car-rental companies? Your first stop should be

RentalCarMomma.com. They collect coupon codes from around the Web and help you find the least expensive options for one-way rentals and rentals in other countries. Another site you can try is RetailMeNot.com/coupons/carrental.

Who Knew? Reader's Tip

Save money on car rentals by not renting at the airport, which charges rental car companies concession fees. Instead, take a cab to a nearby location—even with the fare factored in, you'll be surprised how much you save.

—*Drey Luca, via email*

Travel Savings for Students and Teachers If you're 26 or under, you have all the luck. Not only do your knees never get sore, but you can also get great deals when you're traveling in Europe. If you're age 12–26, if you're a student of any age, or if you're a teacher or faculty member, you qualify for the International Student ID Card. Available at ISECard.com, the card costs $25, but with it you get discounts on trains, rental cars, tourist attractions, and more. Best of all, they'll provide medical travel insurance up to $2,000.

Creative Packing Tips

Pack Alike These days, when we pack, it's all about shoving everything we need into a carry-on to save on checked-bag fees. One rule we live by to make it work? Pack clothes that are in the same color family, and pants that can go with a lot of different shirts. You can more easily mix and match them, so you'll have to pack less. This trick will also come in handy when you spill something on yourself—if your blue shirt is soiled, you still have another in your suitcase.

Camera Saver When packing a camera, place it in a plastic container for bar soap—usually the perfect size for your digital point-and-shoot.

Make Kid Travel Easier If you're traveling with young kids, make it easier to get ready each morning while you're away. When packing their clothes, pack full outfits, and place each one in a big Ziploc bag (with any hair or other accessories)—plus an extra or two for spills and emergencies. Each morning, your child can pick out one Ziploc full of clothes to wear that day. That way, you won't have to spend as much time making sure they look presentable!

Plan Ahead When Packing When packing a suitcase for a trip, put at least one outfit in the suitcase of your spouse (or other travel buddy). If your suitcase gets lost, you'll have at least a few clothes to tide you over until it's found.

Who Knew? Reader's Tip

Save those empty paper towel rolls, and use them while you're packing your suitcase for vacation! Roll your clothes around the paper towel rolls, and you'll help prevent creases. You'll also have a handy spot inside the roll for storing small items like socks and underwear.

—*Lauren Holcomb Wiley, via Facebook*

Do-Ahead Souvenir Saver Protect fragile items, like souvenirs, by thinking ahead before you pack. Fill a few Ziploc bags with packing peanuts or leftover bubble wrap, and toss them in your suitcase. They won't add much weight to the bag, and you'll be really glad you brought them once you find that one-of-a-kind vase or other fragile trinket during your travels.

Send It Ahead Especially when you have a ton of presents to pack, it's usually more frugal to pay to ship the contents of your suitcase to your destination ahead of time. Most airlines charge between $15 and $30 for the first checked bag and much more for the second, while it only costs around $14 to mail up to 70 pounds via the post office.

Clip-Cover Your Razors Here's a clever second use for binder clips: Use them to cover your razors! If you lose the plastic cap that comes with many brands of razors, simply open up the clip, stick the razor head inside the plastic base, and set the clip's metal prongs back down in place. It's perfect for traveling because it keeps the blade safe while still allowing air to circulate so that moisture doesn't get trapped.

While You're Away...

Put Your Plants on Autopilot If you are going on a long vacation and are unable to find someone to care for your plants, place a large container of water near your plant (if you have several, gather them into one spot to make it easy). Then place one end of a long piece of yarn into the water, and stick the other end into the plant's soil, near the roots. Lay the strand across the stalks of the plant. This will keep it moist until you return. You can also poke a small hole in the side of a plastic bottle, fill it with water, and place it in the soil next to your plant. The slow drip keeps the plants watered slowly but continuously.

Keep Burglars Away If you're concerned about your house being broken into while you're away, don't stop at automatic light switches. Ask your neighbor to park his car in your driveway, so robbers will think someone's at home.

Save While You're Away Many newspapers and magazines will allow you to suspend your home delivery or subscription. If you're going on a long vacation, make sure to call them up and stop service while you're away. You can also often do this for online movie rental and other services. You won't miss them while you're gone, and then you'll get an extra week or two when your subscription would normally be up.

Be a Clever Traveler

Dealing with Dry Air in Hotels Here's an ingenious travel trick if you're staying at a hotel and find that the air in your room is too dry for your comfort. Just fill the bathtub with warm water and leave the bathroom door open. It will help add humidity to the air in the entire room.

A New Purpose for the TV One of the most frustrating things you can do is to forget your phone chargers when you're traveling. From experience, we've learned that most televisions in hotels have small USB ports on their sides. If you have a USB cord but no wall socket, you can often just plug your phone into the TV and watch it charge. Problem solved!

Who Knew? Reader's Tip

When booking a hotel for your vacation, make sure to choose one that offers a free breakfast and an in-room refrigerator and microwave. Eating a couple of meals at the hotel is one of the easiest ways to save while you're away.

—*Rita Guerrero, via email*

Protect an Underwater Camera Yes, the housing on your underwater camera will prevent moisture damage, but condensation can still fog or smear the lens, which might result in blurry photos and even corrosion. To fix this, slip one or two packets of silica gel inside the casing with your camera before bringing it underwater. The silica gel draws out excess moisture, keeping your camera dry and in good working condition.

Who Knew? Reader's Tip

Whenever we're traveling, we like having some extra cash on us in the event our debit cards don't work, or we can't find an ATM, etc. But carrying too much cash can be nerve-wracking, especially when traveling abroad. We travel with "secret" money by saving old lip balm containers. When they're empty, rinse them out, then roll up a paper towel and clean the inside. They're the perfect size to hold some rolled-up bills right in your pocket or purse, and no one would ever guess!

—*Julie Dennison, via Facebook*

Plug the Socket It's impossible to carry an entire baby-proofing kit with you every time you travel, but you can put a literal Band-Aid on the situation in hotel rooms: Use Band-Aids to cover open outlets! You'll still need to keep an eye on babies and toddlers playing nearby to make sure they don't peel them off, but will at least have the peace of mind knowing that the outlets aren't left bare.

Camera, Where's My Car? Long-term parking at the airport is convenient, but after a busy vacation it can be impossible to remember where you parked! Make it easier by snapping a picture of your row and aisle with your digital camera. When it's time to find your car, go back to the first photo you took to remember where it is!

Don't Stand in Line If you've been to an airport lately, you've probably noticed that the ticket counters are staffed by fewer people than ever before. It's annoying on a regular travel day, but if there are lots of flight cancellations, this can mean a two-hour-plus wait in line. Save yourself a lot of time by skipping the line all together. Instead, call the customer service number for your airline and rebook your cancelled flight right over the phone.

Saving Money on Road Trips

How Much Will Gas Cost? Planning a road trip? Find out exactly how much you need to budget for gas money at FuelCostCalculator.com. Enter the make and model of your car and your starting and destination cites, and AAA will calculate how much it will cost you using the Environmental Protection Agency's fuel economy ratings and its own gasoline prices report. With rising gas prices and fluctuating airfare, this is a great site to visit if you're not sure taking the car will save you money.

How to Find Cheap Gas If you have a smartphone, the GasBuddy app is a must before you hit the road. It will pinpoint your location and let you know the least expensive pump prices nearby. You'll often find that the gas stations closest to the highway are more expensive than the ones a bit off your course, so use the app to find one off the beaten path and you could save as much as a dollar per gallon or more.

Road Trip Entertainment Never have to worry about what your kids are going to do in the car again with Rad Road Trips. At their site, you can download free activity books for kids especially designed to keep them entertained in the car. The site also has individual coloring pages and a maze generator.

Who Knew? Reader's Tip

Help keep the "are-we-there-yet?" complaints to a minimum on road trips! Make this easy toy with some hot glue, magnets, and a cookie sheet. Glue the magnets to the back of puzzle pieces, then stick them onto the cookie sheet for a jigsaw puzzle your kids can do in the car.

—*Caroline Marie Wanat, via WhoKnewTips.com*

The Family Overnight Bag If you're traveling by car and will be spending a single night at a hotel, consider packing a separate bag for this night only. Have everyone in your family add their items to that bag, and it will be the only one you'll have to pull out of the car on your layover.

Go Long Instead of making a lot of short stops for the kids on road trips, consider taking two or three long stops instead. Parks and tourist attractions allow kids time to run around (and get tired), and can help reduce the amount you spend—because every time you stop means more souvenirs, food, or other items your kids may want.

Saving Money on Family Activities

TV: Live and In-Person! If you live near a big city, especially Los Angeles or New York, one of the most fun free activities you can do is attend a free TV taping. Talk shows, sitcoms, and game shows are always looking for studio audience members, and it's not only a blast to see a show live, but also to get a peek at what happens behind the scenes. To get tickets to shows, visit TVTickets.com for shows in LA, or NYCGo.com for events and shows in New York (click on "TV show tapings" under "Top attractions."). If a show you know and like is being taped in your area, try looking for it or its network online or seeing if there is a phone number at the end of the show to call for audience tickets.

For Do-It-Yourself Kids At the Home Depot's Kids Workshops, you and your child can build fun projects like toolboxes, fire trucks, mail organizers, birdhouses, and bug containers. The workshops are free, designed for kids 5–12, and usually occur once a month in all Home Depot stores. These fantastic classes not only give you a fun activity to share with your kid (adult participation is required), they also teach skills and give you a few freebies to take with you. Find out more at Workshops.HomeDepot.com. Lowe's has similar how-to clinics for kids; get the details at LowesBuildAndGrow.com.

Let's Go to the Circus! According to Ringling Bros. and Barnum & Bailey, "Parenthood brings many wonderful firsts—your baby's first tooth, your baby's first steps . . . and of course, your baby's first circus!" If you have a child who is under one year of age, sign up to get a free circus ticket that never expires! Just go to Ringling.com and click on "Special offers," where you'll find the "Baby's first circus" offer as well as other discount promotions.

Visiting Museums for Free Even if they normally have high admission prices, most museums offer opportunities for you to visit for free. If a museum gets money from the government, it's usually required to either offer free admission one day a week or to charge admission as a "suggested donation"—that is, you only have to pay what you want. Other museums have late hours that are free to visitors once a week or month. If you like looking at art, also check out galleries, where you can find cool, local art displayed for free in the hopes that someone will buy it.

Save This Summer For ideas on fun, free activities to do over the summer, try checking out your community center

SAVING AT THEME PARKS

Call Ahead Heading to a theme park this summer? The first thing you should do is call them. Most parks (or their auto-mated representative) will tell you about current deals being offered, and may offer promotions of their own. Also check the website of the individual park you're visiting.

Gather Up Your Friends Headed to Six Flags or another theme park or attraction? Go with a bigger group and you could get a discount. If you have at least 15 people in your party, you can usually get a good deal, depending on the time of year. Just call up the park or visit their website to see if they offer group discounts.

Use Your Connections A lot of organizations offer discount packages to local and national theme parks. Check with any organizations to which you belong to see if you can save, such as the AARP, AAA, wholesale clubs like BJ's or Costco, or a branch of the military. Also look for promotions mailed out with your credit card bill.

Pack Your Lunch Before you get to the theme park, consider the real money-wasters: food and drinks, which are marked up sky-high. Bring lunches from home, and be willing to go back out to the parking lot and eat in the car if you can't bring them into the park.

or park district. Most towns have tons of free summertime events, from sports clinics for kids to free concerts for adults. See if they have a website or pick up a calendar at your local branch.

Who Knew? Reader's Tip

When you're headed to the beach, make sure to keep your electronics in plastic freezer bags. Sand can easily get inside them, so the plastic makes the perfect see-through barrier.

—*Becca Luechauer, via Facebook*

Beach Towel Clincher When you're headed to the beach, make sure to take some hair clips with you (the kind that look like a couple of claws). They're perfect for securing towels around your swimsuit or even to your beach chair. Of course, you can also use large binder clips, but they're not quite as chic!

Solve a Suntan-Oil Spill You had a great time at the beach, but you accidentally got suntan lotion all over your cover-up. To remove this stubborn stain, cover with liquid dish detergent and rub in. Then turn your kitchen sink on at full blast and run under cold water.

For the Ski Buff Like skiing? You'll love Liftopia.com. It offers discounts on lift tickets for more than 100 ski resorts across the United States and Canada. You can search by destination or by categories like "good for beginners" and "nighttime skiing." You can also sign up for an email newsletter that will let you know about upcoming deals.

Because a Good Game Is a Good Game If you love going to see sports, but don't love the price tag of taking your whole family to a professional game, consider amateur sports instead. Colleges as well as intramural leagues have games every weekend for free or a couple of dollars. It's great to support local teams, and younger kids won't even know the difference in skill between a pro player and a Division Three league anyway.

Free Night at the Movies These days, it costs a small fortune to take your family to the movies. But at FilmMetro.com, you can get free tickets to advanced screenings and movies that have just been released! Search by city, or browse current listings. The pickings here are often slim, but the site gives you a sneak peek at future offerings, so if you make it a habit to check back often, you may be able to snag free tickets to the latest blockbuster.

Free Movie and Game Rentals Our favorite place to rent movies and video games is through Redbox, which has kiosks at various stores for easy rental and return. Their rental prices are less than two dollars for DVDs—as long as you return them the next day. To find a Redbox location near you or to reserve a DVD before you show up, simply visit Redbox.com. While you're there, make sure to sign up for email alerts and/or text messages to receive occasional promo codes for free rentals! You can also try Googling "Redbox coupon codes" to see if people have posted recent codes online.

Plan on Souvenirs No matter where you go on your family adventure, you know your kids are going to ask for souvenirs, so figure out a plan before you go. Give each child a certain amount they are allowed to spend on gift shop items for the whole day. For more indecisive kids afraid of hitting their limit, make sure to offer them the chance to go back for an item in a store if they don't find anything they like more (ours usually do).

Who Needs Rentals When You Have Friends? The easiest place to get free DVDs may be at the homes of your friends! Try starting a movie-lending circle with friends or neighbors who also watch a lot of movies. Each person has another person they give movies to, and someone they receive them from. When you get your own movie back, it's time to pick a new one! You may want to pick a timeframe to exchange the movie—for example, sometime before each weekend or at a weekly book club or school-related meeting. Movie-lending circles are a great way to discover movies you might not have picked out yourself, but really enjoy.

Who Knew? Reader's Tip

Headed to a zoo or another local attraction? If there's a hotel nearby, you may want to stop by their lobby, and not just for a bathroom break. Many hotels carry brochures for sites popular with tourists, and many of those brochures have coupons! Take a peek inside to see if you can save.
—*Bill Abramoff, via WhoKnewTips.com*

See a Movie for Free Many museums and colleges over free screenings of films. Sure, they're not the latest big releases, but if you're in the mood for a classic or artsy flick, check and see if they are offered nearby. Many facilities even have full-sized screens in auditoriums. And they won't get angry if you sneak in your own candy!

chapter 6

Saving on Holidays and Parties

For Fabulous Party Food

Party Potables

Fun Tricks for Kids' Parties

Picnics and Barbecues

DIY Party Decorations

Sweet Savings on Valentine's Day

Love-of-the-Irish Ideas
for St. Patrick's Day

For Fabulous Party Food

Food Count Wondering how much food to make for your big soiree? Wonder no longer. At a cocktail party (no dinner served), 10–12 bite-size portions per person is a good bet. If you're also serving a meal, figure on 4–5 bites per guest. For dip, figure 2 tablespoons per person (plus veggies or crackers for dipping), and for cheese, get 4 ounces for each person.

Who Knew? Reader's Tip

The next time you're hosting a buffet but don't have a big budget, try this caterer's secret. Place the more inexpensive items—like bread, salad, and pasta—at the beginning of the buffet line. That way, the guests' plates will be mostly full once they get to the end of the line, where the expensive meats are placed, and they'll take a smaller portion—saving you a bundle!
                            —*Melanie Lusser Reid, via Facebook*

Hot Cross Buns Having a dinner party? Here's a great tip for keeping dinner rolls warm long after they've come out of the oven. When you put the rolls in the oven to bake, add a ceramic tile too. By the time the rolls are done, the tile will be (very!) hot. Place it in the basket and put your rolls on top; the tile will keep them warm. You can also use aluminum foil instead of the tile, but it won't retain the heat as long.

The Secret to Day-Ahead Salad It's so much easier to prepare food a day ahead for a dinner party—but what to do about the salad? Making the salad before guests arrive usually leads to a soggy mess, but here's a tip to allow you to make the salad in advance without it going soft. Gather lettuce and any of the following ingredients: broccoli, cabbage, carrots, cauliflower, celery, cucumbers, onions, peppers, and radishes. Chop them up and place them in a large bowl. Then completely cover all your ingredients with water and keep the bowl in the refrigerator until you need it. On the day of the party, drain the ingredients in a colander, and spin in a salad spinner. Finally, add tomatoes, croutons, and any other toppings and enjoy a crisp, delicious salad.

Keep Fruit Looking Fresh Even though the taste isn't affected, it's still disappointing to unveil your fruit salad only to discover a thin layer of brown oxidation all over the fruit. A common method for keeping cut fruit looking fresh is to add a bit of lemon juice. However, an even more

BIRTHDAY CAKE TRICKS

Skewer Your Cake and Eat It Too If you're having a problem keeping a layer cake together when you're icing it, stick a few bamboo skewers into the cake through both layers; remove them as you're frosting the top.

The Icing on the Cake To keep a cake from sliding around on the plate as you're icing it, place a dab of frosting in the middle of the plate before you place the cake on top. The icing will keep the cake in place, and no one will notice the little bit of extra frosting on the bottom.

Crumb-Free Cake Frosting Don't let crumbs turn your smooth icing into a lumpy mess! The secret that many pastry chefs use is to dollop spoonfuls of icing a couple of inches apart all over the top of the cake, and then use a spatula to simply spread them out.

Icing Guide This bakers' trick makes decorating a cinch! With a toothpick, trace the pattern, picture, or lettering before you pipe the icing. This guide will help you make fewer mistakes.

Smooth Slicing If you've got a delicate cake that will fall apart and stick to the knife when you cut it, use dental floss—yes, dental floss—to slice it. Hold the floss tight and give it a slight sawing motion as you move it down to cut through the cake.

effective method is to fill a spray bottle with water and a few dissolved vitamin C tablets (usually available in the vitamin and nutritional supplement section of your drug store). Spray this mixture on the cut fruit and not only will you stop the oxidation, you'll be getting added vitamins!

Keep Food Fresh To keep meat or cheese hors d'oeuvres moist, cover them with a damp paper towel, then cover loosely with plastic wrap. Many fillings (as well as bread) dry out very quickly, but with this tip, you can make these simple appetizers first and have them ready on the table when guests arrive.

For Cones that Don't Drip Keep ice-cream cones leak-free with this simple tip: Place a miniature marshmallow or chocolate kiss in the bottom of the cone before adding the ice cream. Either can help prevent the tip of the cone from leaking—and you'll get a delicious treat at the end of the cone!

Make Ice Cream Shapes Here's a fun and unique way to serve ice cream next to cake. Buy a pint-size container of your favorite ice cream, then slice right through it (cardboard and all) with a serrated knife, making ice cream "rounds" that are about 1-inch thick. Peel off the remaining cardboard, then use cookie cutters to make various shapes. Store them in your freezer between pieces of parchment paper until you're ready to serve. And if you don't use the entire pint, the top will still sit flush against your "short stack" to keep it fresh for later.

Party Potables

• •

Pick a Cocktail, Any Cocktail One of the biggest costs of any party is the alcohol. To keep your booze bill in check, don't load up on every kind of liquor in the store. Instead, serve a single special cocktail. Be creative! You can serve mojitos in August, and a delicious mulled wine come December. Not only will it reduce your expenses, but you'll also set the tone for the party, creating a more memorable experience for your guests!

Frugal Boozing No gathering is complete at our house without family, friends, fun, and lots of refreshing good-time beverages. (Translation: beer.) Keep an eye out for sales on beer and wine, which usually start on the Sunday or Wednesday before a holiday. Or, just head on over to SaveOnBrew.com, a site that locates beer sales in your neighborhood. Just enter your zip code and, voilà, up-to-the-minute discounts!

Ice Cube Math If you run out of ice at a party, you're in trouble! But how do you know how much to buy? Use this simple metric. If you're serving mostly cocktails, the average person at a party will go through 10–15 cubes. When you buy ice cubes in a bag, you will get about 10 cubes per pound.

Who Knew? Reader's Tip

Serving bottled beer at your party? Here's a clever life hack that will impress your friends: Offer each drinker a matchstick along with the brew. If you place one matchstick over the mouth of the bottle, you'll prevent the beer from going flat.
—*Jason Amburgy, via WhoKnewTips.com*

Party Planning Whether you're serving Coke or cocktails at a party, it's a good idea to have plenty of drinks on hand for your guests. Here's a good rule of thumb: Plan on two drinks per person for the first hour, then one drink per person per hour after that. For a long party, estimate around five drinks per person.

Filtering Your Wine Red wines that are more than eight years old tend to develop sediment. It's harmless, but it doesn't always look too nice. Get rid of sediment, and any bits of cork, by pouring your wine through a coffee filter and into a decanter before you serve it.

Easily Label Drinks Keep a handle on whose drink is whose by pressing window decals onto the sides of glassware. This is a perfect trick for a party that takes place around a holiday, when you can use festive decals that are easy to find at party stores.

Who Knew? Reader's Tip

Having a party? Put your child's inexplicable Silly Bandz obsession to good use! These rubber bands in fun shapes are perfect for putting around the stems of wine glasses so your guests can tell whose are whose. —*Brenda Morgano, via Facebook*

Re-Fizz Champagne Champagne lost its fizz? Place a raisin in the glass and the last bits of carbon dioxide that remain will cling to the raisin, then be released again as bubbles. You can also try throwing a few raisins into the bottle before you make the final pour.

Fizzy Fun For a snazzy party treat, add some color and sweetness to champagne. First color some granulated sugar by adding a few drops of food coloring to it. Then wet the rim of each champagne glass and press into the sugar to give it a sweet, colorful rim—perfect for guests who find champagne a little too dry.

Who Knew? Reader's Tip

Wondering what to do with leftover wine (besides drinking it, of course)? Keep it fresh by putting whatever is left in a small container such as a jam jar. This limits the amount of air the wine is put in contact with, keeping it fresh. That's the same thing those expensive wine vacuum sealers do, so save your money and do this instead!

—*Amy Hardaloupas, via Facebook*

No-Spill Party Drinks We love anything that gives us more time to talk to our company and cuts down on hosting duties during a party. One simple way to hand out drinks: Use muffin trays instead of flat trays. You can easily carry two dozen glasses without breaking a sweat, and even younger family members will be able to help.

Egg Carton Ice Cubes If you're having a party or your family just seems to go through a lot of icy beverages in the summer, stock up on ice cubes now! Use plastic or

Styrofoam egg cartons as makeshift ice trays by filling each eggcup with water. You can even close the lid and stack them on top of each other!

....

Be Creative with Ice If you're serving punch at a party, pour some of it into ice cube trays and freeze. This way, you can keep the punch nice and cold without diluting it. This also works well with wine, iced tea, or any number of other beverages.

Who Knew? Reader's Tip

It's nice to keep an ice bucket next to your drinks on the table, but once the ice melts you're left with a few cubes soaking in a puddle of water. To fix this problem, place a colander on the top of your ice bucket and fill *it* with the ice. Water will drip through the bottom, and the ice will be easier to grab with some tongs.

—*Cynthia Ferris, via WhoKnewTips.com*

Flower Power When it comes to entertaining, it's the details that make the party special. That's why we love this creative idea for ice cubes. Place edible flowers (like violets, pansies, or impatiens) in ice cube trays, fill with water, and freeze. Then use the flower-filled cubes to make a specialty cocktail or any other drink look incredibly elegant. You can also use the leaves from herbs like mint and rosemary.

Fun Tricks for Kids' Parties

Sundae Fun Repurpose a plastic ice cube tray by making it into a killer sundae station. Use the various compartments for nuts, crushed cookies, candy, and other toppings, then serve with ice cream and let the kids make their own sundaes. (Don't be surprised if they dump everything on top.)

Wiggly Jell-O Worms For a child's party treat that will win raves, use bendy straws to make Jell-O worms! In addition to the straws, you'll also need a tall, slim container (such as a quart container from milk or juice) to stand the straws up on their ends while the Jell-O is firming up. Pack the straws inside as tightly as possible, adding more straws until they're all standing up on their ends—we ended up using more than 100 straws. Then, make some Jell–O as specified on the package directions (we used two boxes of lime flavor), mixing together the Jell–O powder with gelatin and boiling water. When the mixture has cooled so that it's just barely warm, stir in ⅔ cup heavy cream for every 1 box of Jell–O you used. Now it's time to pour the mixture into the straws! Take your time and consider yourself skilled if you only spill on the counter once. After sticking in the refrigerator until they're firm, remove the "worms" by holding the straws over a colander and running under warm water. They should slither right out!

Who Knew? Reader's Tip

Did you know that many grocery stores offer a free cake for a baby's first birthday? It's as easy as going to your supermarket's bakery section and asking! Even if they don't advertise the offer, many supermarkets will provide you with a free birthday cake as long as you order it in advance. Some may also ask to see a copy of your baby's birth certificate to make sure your request is legit.

—Alex Boydston, via Facebook

Get Creative with Cake Little kids usually end up eating cake with their hands anyway, so try this fun dessert treat: Place flat-bottomed ice-cream cones in a high-sided baking pan and fill them two-thirds full with cake batter. Bake them at 325° for 30 minutes, and once they cool you can hold your cake and eat it, too!

Cream-Filled Cupcakes Add a delicious surprise to your birthday cupcakes this year: a creamy center. It's easier than you think! Once your cupcakes are baked and cooled, poke a hole through the top of each one with a straw. Scoop the frosting of your choice into a plastic Ziploc bag, then seal it up. Slice a small hole in one corner so you can pipe your frosting through the top of your cupcakes. When you're finished piping, spread frosting over the tops to cover the holes, or hide them with a chocolate chip or other candy.

Who Knew? Reader's Tip

We love making Jell-O Jigglers for kids' party snacks—they're easy, sweet, and fun to eat. The best part? Jell-O pieces can take so many different forms! For your next batch, use your child's Duplos or Mega Bloks as molds (just be sure to wash them first!). Kids will love their edible "toys"!

—*Ashley Wampler, via Facebook*

How to Carry Cupcakes Turn a shirt-box into the perfect cupcake carrier. Cut eight *X*s equidistant from each other in the lid, then place the lid on top of the box. The cupcake bottoms will fit snugly into each *X*, making them easy to take with you.

SAVING ON KIDS' PARTIES

Cue the Cupcakes Here's a simple saver for a child's birthday: Consider serving cupcakes instead of one large cake, which will eliminate the need for forks and paper plates—and save you money.

Party Like It's Wednesday Night If your children's birthday parties are putting a hurt on your budget, there's a simple solution—have the party during the week instead of on a weekend. If it's possible for you, you can save big by having the party midweek—so much so that it's worth it the extra hassle of arranging to pick up a dozen extra kids when you pick yours up from school.

Head to Colleges for Help If you're hosting a party that requires you to hire someone like a clown, face painter, or magician, head to your local college first. There, you'll find hundreds of young people who will do the job for a lot less than a pro. Put up an ad near the cafeteria, and stop by the career office to see if they have an online bulletin board.

For Bigger Birthday Bashes Thinking about throwing your child's birthday party in a larger venue? Contact local toddler co-ops and daycare centers to see if you can rent out their space on the weekend—some organizations offer fantastic rates!

On-the-Spot Marshmallow Topping Need a quick, delicious topping for your party cupcakes? Try this: During the final few minutes of baking time, place one large marshmallow on top of each cupcake. As the cooking continues, the marshmallows will melt into a sweet, sticky frosting—they're done when the tops become lightly browned.

All's Fair in Love and Piñatas When it comes to piñatas, the spoils go to the bullies, but not if you separate the candies and prizes into Ziploc bags for each guest before stuffing them inside the papier-mâché animal. The kids will still get a rush of excitement when the piñata drops, but the game won't dissolve into an "Are we having fun yet?" moment when they start fighting over Tootsie Rolls and Milky Ways.

Bowling Party in the Backyard! If your kids love to bowl as much as ours do, this party will be a memorable hit! On flat ground, create a bowling lane with different-colored party streamers. For the pins, collect 10 plastic bottles filled with water, and drop a bit of food coloring in each. Arrange the pins in proper formation at the end of the bowling lane. Use a soccer ball or basketball as your bowling ball and get your kids ready to score!

Picnics and Barbecues

Makeshift Platter If you're looking for a platter for deviled eggs, brownies, or other picnic items, simply cover a piece of corrugated cardboard with aluminum foil (dull side up). It might not be fancy, but you can simply recycle it when you're finished—no mess!

Clever Condiment Tray Preparing condiments for a barbecue? Use a muffin tin! It's the perfect size for toppings like chopped onions, relish, shredded lettuce, pickles, and more. Plus, you'll only have one dish to wash.

Free On-the-Fly Picnic Blanket Maybe it's because we have so many pictures of our kids wrapped in them on family vacations, but beach towels are one of those items that we hate throwing away or using as rags once they get old. If you have four or more towels that are getting too old to use at the pool, turn them into a giant, use-anywhere blanket for picnics, outdoor concerts, or family events. Just sew the edges of the towels together, and you're done! Then bundle up your on-the-fly (and free!) blanket and stick it in the trunk. You'll have it at the ready for future family excursions.

For the Fastest Cold Beer The best way to chill beer or soda rapidly is to fill a cooler with layers of water, ice, and salt, then plunge the beers inside. In about 20 minutes or less, the beer will be ice cold! Even if the ice water is warmer than your freezer, it absorbs the warmth from the bottles or cans more rapidly and more efficiently than the cold air of the freezer does.

Who Knew? Reader's Tip

Keep your picnic tablecloth in place on windy days by using clothespins: Hot glue one clothespin underneath each corner of the table. Clip the ends of the tablecloth into the pins, and those wind gusts will be no match for your party!

—*Karen Glinksi, via Facebook*

Coal for Coolers To keep your cooler fresh and odor free, throw in 10–15 charcoal briquettes, close the top, and leave it overnight. In the morning, clean the cooler with soapy water, and it will smell like new.

Six-Pack Containers Six-packs are a must-have at a barbecue—and not just for the beer. Turn an old six-pack container into a holder and carrier for condiments like ketchup, mustard, and relish. You can even stick napkins and plastic utensils inside. To make it extra strong (and waterproof), wrap in duct tape!

....

BBQ Squeeze If you have your own special recipe for barbecue or hot sauce, it's probably a must-have at every 'que. The perfect container for storing and dispensing it is a water bottle with a squirt top. Buy water in one of these types of bottles at the store for a container that's easy to toss out; or use a reusable one with your favorite team's logo when tailgating or watching the game at home.

....

A Tasty Grill To help reduce smoke and improve the flavor of food on your grill, use an onion! Cut a red onion in half, pierce it with a fork, and dip in water. Then use the onion half to wipe down the grill rack. It will clean the grill rack and leave a tasty flavor behind!

....

Easy Fish on the Grill If you have two small wire racks, you can easily cook a fish on your outdoor grill (and impress your friends). First, find toaster oven or cooling racks and some fireproof wire. Oil the racks, then put the fish between them and tie the racks together. Grill the fish on one side, then flip your newly constructed basket with large tongs or a spatula. This makeshift cage will keep delicate fish from breaking apart.

....

For Super Steak If you're grilling a steak on a closed barbecue, here's a neat trick your guests will love. Open a can of beer and place it on the hottest part of the grill. It will boil and keep the meat moist, while adding flavor, too.

Succulent Grilled Corn There's nothing more delicious than perfectly juicy corn on the cob straight off the grill. To keep the corn from drying out during cooking, we leave the husks intact the entire time—this keeps the moisture in, ensuring that our corn is steamed and juicy. First, stick the cobs in a bowl or sink filled with cold water; let them soak for 15 minutes. Then place them on the grill, still unshucked. Grill until tender, turning occasionally, about 20 minutes. When you're ready to dig in, pull the husks and silks back to the ends of the cob and use them as handles.

Today's News: A Clean Grill! A great way to clean your barbecue grill is with wet newspaper. After cooking, just place it on a warm grill for one hour with the lid closed. You'll be amazed how easily the grime comes off!

Firmer Gelatin If you've ever had a Jell-O salad melt at a picnic, you'll love this tip. When you add the water to any gelatin recipe in hot summer months, mix in a teaspoon of white vinegar to keep salads and desserts firm.

Picnic Preservative Preparing food for a picnic? It may surprise you to learn you should use more mayo! In addition to being delicious, the silky condiment also has bacteria-fighting acids! Of course, food poisoning is always a risk at picnics, but you shouldn't be afraid of adding more mayo to your favorite dishes. Just don't leave foods out in the hot sun, and keep lids on whenever possible.

Who Knew? Reader's Tip

Coleslaw is one of our summertime faves, but the shredded cabbage salad always tends to turn soggy and limp before we've made it to a second helping. Luckily, we've found a prep tip that helps keep cabbage crunchy for longer: Place a head of cabbage in a large bowl or pot, fill it with ice-cold water, then add 1 tablespoon salt for every two quarts water. Let soak for 10 minutes. The cabbage absorbs water, helping it stay hydrated and crisp even once it's shredded and mixed into a salad.

—*Angela Toffolo, via Facebook*

Just Say No to Lighter Fluid When the coals start to die down on your grill, don't squirt them with more lighter fluid, which not only costs money but can leave your food tasting bad (not to mention, burn the hair off your arm). Instead, blow a hair dryer on the base of the coals. The hair dryer acts as a pair of bellows, and your fire will be going again in no time.

See Also . . . For tips about keeping bugs away from your picnic or barbecue, see the Practically Free Pest Control chapter.

DIY Party Decorations

Brighten a Backyard You're hosting a backyard party that's turned into an evening affair. Unfortunately, your outdoor accent lights aren't bright enough, but you don't want to have to turn on the glaring light by your door. Instead, fold pieces of aluminum foil in half (shiny side out) and wrap like a bowl around the bottom of the light, then attach with a few pieces of electrical tape. The foil will reflect the light in a nice, shimmering pattern.

Put a Cork on It For your next dinner party, make elegant place markers out of leftover wine corks. After polishing off enough bottles of wine to have a cork for each seat at your table, you'll also need some blank place cards, sandpaper, and a utility blade or X-Acto knife. First, sand down one side of the cork so that it lays flat on a table.

Then, using the utility blade or X-Acto knife, cut a slit on the opposite side of the cork, along its entire length. You'll want a cut about ¼-inch deep, so that it can support the card. Finally, insert the place cards, and set the corks on the table for your party!

Showcase Table Centerpieces Does your centerpiece get lost among salad bowls and turkey platters? To make it really stand out and beautify your dining table, prop it on top of several upside-down plastic cups.

Party Lights If you have a hula-hoop and some icicle Christmas lights, you can create a beautiful, chandelier-like lighting fixture for an evening outdoor party that will win you glowing reviews! (Yes, the pun was intended.) First, you'll want to spray paint the hula-hoop a dark color, preferably black, so that it's virtually invisible in the dark. Then wrap a strand or two of the icicle lights around it and suspend it outside where you'll be throwing the party. The lights will lend a magical glow to your get-together.

Jar Displays Have some beautiful clear jars, but don't know what to do with them? Try putting photos inside! Add marbles, rocks, colored sand, or other decoration at the bottom, then bend the photo ever-so-slightly so it fits the curve of the jar. This is a great idea for birthday or an-

CLEVER
CANDLE TRICKS

Candlestick Fit Most taper candles are too large to fit into standard candlesticks, so you'll have to do a little work to ensure your candle fits securely. (Do not light the candle and melt wax into the base—this is messy and dangerous!) First, try placing the candle base under hot water; this softens the wax and allows it to mold to its new surroundings. If this doesn't do the trick, whittle down the wax around the base of the candle with a paring knife, checking the fit as you go.

Any Candle in Any Candlestick If your candle is too skinny for your candlestick, wrap some aluminum foil around the base of it until you get a snug fit.

Making Candles Drip-Free Store your candles in the freezer. Once you light them, they'll go hours before they start dripping.

Keep Candleholders Clean To prevent wax from sticking to a candleholder, rub a thin coat of olive oil on the base of the holder before lighting the candle.

Candle Scandal Candle accident? Removing wax from your floor, table, or wall is easy if you soften the wax first with a blow dryer, then peel it off. Wipe any excess with a paper towel, and then clean with a mixture of half white vinegar and half water.

niversary parties. Put pictures of the honorees in the jars and you have some unique centerpieces!

Who Knew? Reader's Tip

Don't shell out cash at the hardware store for outdoor-party accessories like tiki torches and citronella candles. Instead, first check discount stores like Marshalls, which offer overstock merchandise for much less. You can often find citronella products, plastic dinnerware sets, and picnic napkins for a fraction of the cost!

—*Susan Milan, via WhoKnewTips.com*

Birthday Photo Collage We love this creative idea for jazzing up party decor. Collect all the photographs you can find that celebrate your guest of honor—from babyhood, childhood, school yearbooks, vacations, and other memorable events. Then compile them into a large wall collage: Arrange the photos into giant numbers to mark the person's age or year of birth, spell out a name or meaningful word or phrase, or simply form a fun shape.

Easy Balloon Garlands Balloon garlands are an inexpensive way to add festive fun to a party. And believe it or not, the easiest way to make one is with a needle! Using fishing line (or thread), run the needle through the tied-off ends of the balloons as close to the knot as possible. We love letting our kids come up with their own color combinations, but you could also do black and orange balloons for Halloween, red and green for Christmas, blue for Hanukkah, and so forth.

Glossy, Decorative Leaves For an easy decorating project, gloss colorful autumn leaves. The whole family can collect them together and spread them out on newspaper inside. To gloss, combine equal parts milk and water and paint over the leaves or brush over with a clean rag. When the leaves are dry, use them to adorn indoor plants, fill a vase with them for an eye-catching centerpiece, spread them out on the mantel, or place them underneath candles to catch the drips.

Rainbow Bright You don't need to be Martha Stewart to create this adorable centerpiece that will liven up any holiday celebration or party. Gather together several bud vases, and fill them with water. In each vase, put a drop or two of food coloring in different colors, and then insert a single flower. You could use a whole rainbow of dyes for a spring get-together, reds and greens for Christmas, pinks and reds for Valentine's Day, and so on. Set the centerpiece out on the table for your guests to enjoy.

Sweet Savings on Valentine's Day

It's All About the Love Valentine's Day doesn't have to be expensive. Sometimes, showing your sweetheart you love them is as easy as telling them so. Write a quick love message on a Post-it note and leave it where your lover will see it first thing in the morning, like on the bathroom mirror. For something more special, compose a letter where you tell your valentine just how much you care, and hand-write it for that personal touch.

Balloon Canopy Bed Celebrate your relationship by making a balloon display above your bed. Get one balloon for each year or month you've been together, and attach a note to each one containing a memory you've shared or a place you've visited as a couple. The colors of the balloons floating above you will create a unique, romantic ambience.

Mix Tape Love Even if you haven't made someone a mix tape since high school, handpicked tunes are a great, free Valentine's treat. Make a custom, romantic playlist to show your sweetie you care! If music isn't your thing, photocopy some of your favorite short stories or poems to present to your loved one as a "literary playlist."

Put a Little Love in a Jar Bring some sweetness to your table by placing candy hearts in a vase or Mason jar. Bonus? The candies never grow stale, so you can save this sweet showpiece for next year, too.

Who Knew? Reader's Tip

If you're sending flowers for a special occasion, skip the national delivery services and websites. Instead, find a flower shop that is local to the recipient and call them directly. Most national services simply charge you a fee, then contact these very same stores themselves.

—*Rupal Patel, via WhoKnewTips.com*

Sweetheart Stencil For an ultra-romantic touch on a baked treat, create a sweet heart shape with powdered sugar. Fold a sheet of paper in half, and trace one half of a heart shape along the fold. Cut it out and open the paper heart; there's your stencil. Place it on a piece of toast, a cake, or cookies, sprinkle powdered sugar inside it, then lift—a powdered-sugar heart for your sweetheart!

Lunch Is for Lovers, Too! For a little less formality on Valentine's Day, consider taking your sweetie out to a romantic lunch or brunch rather than dinner. Not only will you make it more special by sharing it with fewer people (everyone else will probably be making dinner reservations), the lunch menu is often less expensive.

We Heart Cakes A heart-shaped cake is easier to make than you might think. Simply divide your cake batter between one round pan and one square one. When the cakes are cool, cut the round cake in half. Turn the square cake so it looks like a diamond and set the half-rounds on the two top sides. Voilà!

Heart-Shaped Cupcakes Prefer heart-shaped cupcakes to cakes? We know how to do those, too! Simply place cupcake liners inside a regular tin, then stick a marble or ball of foil between each liner and the tin. This will create a V-shape for the top of the heart. Pour enough batter to fill the liners only slightly more than halfway. (Don't pour too much, or the heart shapes won't come through!) Bake as directed, and decorate as you like.

Baking with Heart Once Christmas is over, snag a bag of tiny candy canes that are on sale and use them for these heart-shaped cupcake toppers. On a nonstick baking sheet, place two candy canes side-by-side and flip one over so their "hooks" and bottom edges are touching, forming a heart. Arrange all candy cane hearts on the baking sheet, then bake at 325° for 3 to 5 minutes. Pinch together to seal, then cool and remove with a spatula. They're perfect for decorating cupcakes on Valentine's Day!

Love-of-the-Irish Ideas for St. Patrick's Day

St. Patty's Free Party Emporium Yep, we said "free"! For adorable holiday decorations that you can print out at home, check out LivingLocurto.com/2012/03/st-patricks-free-printables. You'll find festive signs, bottle wrappers, drink flags, cake toppers, cupcake wrappers, and more!

Bring a Little Irish Luck to Your Doorstep Here's another great holiday project for you and the kids: Turn a plain old flowerpot into an adorable green leprechaun hat. In addition to a clay pot, get some green paint and a paintbrush, a large metal washer (for the buckle), sandpaper to sand down the washer, gold paint, thick black ribbon, and a hot-glue gun. Paint the pot green and set it aside to dry. Sand the washer to make it smooth and ready for painting; paint it completely with gold paint. Once both the pot and washer are dry, use your hot-glue gun to secure the black ribbon around the center of the pot. Glue the washer—or buckle—on top of the ribbon, and your leprechaun hat pot is ready to grow some shamrocks!

Who Knew? Reader's Tip

Bring some Irish spirit to the breakfast table by adding a few drops of green food coloring to pancake or waffle batter. Stir the coloring in gradually until you get the shade of green you want, and prepare as usual.　　　　　　—*Jillian Garvey, via email*

Luck Be a Rainbow Collage There really *is* a pot of gold at the end of the rainbow! At the end of this rainbow, at least. You and the kids can make this simple rainbow collage in a snap—all you'll need are paper plates, scissors, paints in all six colors of a rainbow, cotton balls, white glue, and gold glitter or sparkly paint. Slice a paper plate in half with your scissors, then paint the arches of a rainbow onto one half-circle. Dab a few cotton balls in glue and paste them along the bottom of each arch to form clouds. For the gold treasure, mix the glitter with a bit of glue to make a glittery paste, then paint gold coins near one end of the rainbow.

Shamrock Pepper Stamp Making St. Patty's Day decorations with the kids? To fashion a stamp in the shape of a shamrock, simply cut off the bottom of a bell pepper—voilà! Dip the clover shape in green paint and stamp away!

Corned Beef Cook Test For lip-smacking, perfectly tender corned beef this St. Patrick's Day (or any day), give your meat the fork-slip doneness test: Poke a carving fork into the roast and lift upward slowly and carefully. The fork should slip out of the meat cleanly if it's moist and tender.

Egg-citing Easter Ideas

Easter Egg Hunters If you're hosting an egg hunt for kids of various ages, try color-coding the eggs by age group. Yellow eggs might be hidden in easy-to-find places for the younger kids, while green eggs can be stowed in sneakier spots for the big kids.

Easy Easter Egg Dye Never, ever pay for egg dye! Simply mix ½ cup boiling water with ½ teaspoon white vinegar, and add food coloring until you get a hue you like. For a striped egg even the Easter Bunny would be proud of, wrap tape around the egg before dipping. Once the egg dries, remove the tape, tape over the colored parts, and dip again in a different color. You can also use stickers in the shapes of hearts, stars, and letters.

Who Knew? Reader's Tip

Punch up your Easter eggs this year by applying temporary tattoos in addition to colorful dyes. Your kids will want to put the tats on themselves, too!
—*Micah Porterfield, via Facebook*

Easy Marbled Easter Eggs These eggs are even cooler-looking than other marbled eggs. Rather than dyeing just the outer shell, our food coloring seeps into the shells' cracks to create neat spider-web effects. First, hard-boil your eggs as usual. Once they're cooled, tap each egg on a hard surface to make cracks in the shell—but don't peel! Using a spoon, drip food coloring all over the eggs, and let them dry. Rinse with water and peel the shells. You'll have beautiful marbled eggs that are ready to eat!

Easter Egg Accessory The perfect holder for an Easter egg? The upside-down tops to soda and water bottles! For a little extra flair, glue a piece of Easter ribbon around the outside of them.

Egg Dyeing for Toddlers You might think only older kids can dye Easter eggs, but we started our boys off when they were still in diapers. Give your little helpers a plastic container filled with food coloring, water, and a little vinegar. Let them drop the hard-boiled egg in, help them seal it closed, and tell them to "Shake, shake, shake." Pure magic.

Who Knew? Reader's Tip

Make Easter dinner even more fun for the kids (and big kids, too!) by putting together these adorable table settings that look like carrots. You'll need orange paper dinner napkins, green plastic utensils, and green pipe cleaners. Fold each napkin in half to form a rectangle. Set a plastic spoon, fork, and knife on a bottom corner of each napkin, then roll the utensils up in the napkin. Wrap a couple of pipe cleaners around the top of each rolled-up napkin, and your carrot table settings will be good enough to eat!

—*Janine Ward-Garrett, via WhoKnewTips.com*

Beat-the-Sweets Easter Treat We like to mix up our Easter snacks so the kids aren't eating *only* sugary sweets. This snack is a little more healthful than the usual candy, plus it's super-cute and Easter-colorful. Pour cheesy goldfish crackers into a clear plastic pastry bag and tie the opening closed with green ribbon: You've got a carrot! (At least in shape, if not nutritional value.) If you don't have a pastry bag, you can also use the corner of a sandwich bag and some tape.

....

Berry Cool Easter Baskets Here's another creative tip for putting together cute baskets for the kids: Reuse the colorful berry baskets you find at the grocery store! Attach pipe cleaners on each side of the basket to form a handle, and either tie or glue a small bow to the very top of the handle. Weave colored ribbon through the tiny openings in the basket and secure the ends with glue. Finally, fill it with all sorts of Easter goodies: grass at the bottom, then candy, chocolates, marshmallow Peeps, cookies, and toys!

A Frugal and Fun Fourth

Independence Day Decorative Stars For a little added flair at your Fourth of July shindig, set your table with colorful jars adorned with stars! You'll need a few jars; white sticky glue; red, white, and blue spray paint; and— the secret ingredient—Epsom salts! Using glue, trace a star onto the front of each jar. Dab the still-wet star into a dish of Epsom salts, and set it aside to dry. Spray paint each jar in a different patriotic color; let the paint dry. When you're ready to party, fill each starred jar with napkins, utensils, straws, and anything else your guests will need at the dinner table.

Who Knew? Reader's Tip

Here's a festive way to incorporate some patriotism into your Independence Day snacks: American flag open sandwiches! Spread cream cheese onto two slices of bread, then smear some red jam on top. Line up banana slices to form the stripes, and add blueberries in the top left corner for the stars. America the beautiful (and delicious!).

—*Annie Ortiz, via email*

Land of the Free, Home of the Boozy Do you have some patriotic tipplers joining you for the Fourth? Mix up this tasty summertime cocktail that is sure to whet their whistles: Combine 1 ounce vodka, 1 ounce strawberry schnapps, and 3 ounces club soda. Then top it off with blueberries.

Fourth Decor Celebrate in festive style by making some holiday-themed decorations! If you can find a "4" birthday candle or house number, display it inside a large glass vase. Then fill the vase with red, white, and blue candies, and slip miniature American flags inside.

O Say Can You...Be Careful with Those Sparklers?
It's Fourth of July and time to bust out the legal explosives. Kids love to hold sparklers, but make sure their hands are safe by sticking the sparkler in Play-Doh inside its container, which is the perfect size for the kids to wrap their patriotic hands around.

Spook-tacular Halloween Hints

Make Way for House Ghosts Need some creepy Halloween decorations on the cheap? Of course you do! Here's a super-easy tip for making floating ghosts for the outside of your home: Open a white plastic garbage bag and stuff a balled-up newspaper into the very bottom. Tighten the bag around the ball and tie it closed with a rubber band—this is the ghost's head and neck. Use a black Sharpie to draw a ghoulish face, then hang it in your front yard or near the doorstep to scare trick-or-treating guests.

The Early Ghoul Catches the Worm Just like Christmas, you'll find the best Halloween deals way before the day actually rolls around. But why not start even earlier? During the week after Halloween, most related merchandise is deeply discounted—often 75 percent off! Shopping for costumes and decorations almost a year in advance might sound silly, but you'll save lots of cash, time, and stress prepping for next year.

Add Halloween Atmosphere Adding stretchy cobwebs to the doorjambs and corners of your home is a great way to add Halloween flair to the entire house. Instead of buying the ones packaged as spider webs, though, simply go to a craft store and buy a bag of fiberfill. It's the exact same stuff, and a 16-ounce bag of fiberfill is less than half the cost. You can usually find bags of plastic spider rings for super-cheap at party supply or superstores—add them to the webs and on tables around your house for more atmosphere, and encourage your guests to take them home!

Safe Storage for Vinyl Decals Vinyl stickies look great on windows, doors, and other surfaces around the house. But when you remove them, they tend to wrinkle and stick to themselves, making them unusable for future Halloweens. Prevent damage to your decals by laying

JACK-O'-LANTERN TIPS

Pumpkin Goop Scooper When you're carving your pumpkin, rather than using a spoon or your bare hands to scoop out the goopy insides, try an ice-cream scooper instead! Less labor, less sticky mess, and more time for the actual carving.

Halloween Pumpkin Preserver To keep your pumpkin from getting wrinkled and mushy, spray the inside of the hollowed-out pumpkin with an antiseptic spray, which slows down the bacterial growth and increases the time it takes for the pumpkin to deteriorate. Just make sure no one eats a pumpkin that has been sprayed!

The Ever-Glowing Pumpkin To give your jack-o'-lantern a long-lasting glow that's safer than a candle, use a string of Christmas lights. Coil up the lights and stick them in a clear plastic bag, and place the bag inside the pumpkin. Carve a small hole in the back of your pumpkin to plug the lights into an electrical outlet.

For Pumpkins with Shapes Got cookie cutters on hand? Use them to make cool shapes in your jack-o'-lantern! Hold the cutter against the pumpkin's shell, and use a rubber mallet to hit it softly until it penetrates—the cutter should enter at least halfway through the shell. Pull out the cutter, then trace the shape with a small serrated knife to remove the image from the shell.

them flat on a sheet of aluminum foil; then top them with another sheet of foil and fold the edges over to protect them. Store the decals flat with your other Halloween decorations, and they'll be in great shape for next year.

Glowing Ghost Eyes Scaring trick-or-treaters is a huge part of the fun at our house. This super-simple outdoor prop is a doozy! Trace two eyes onto a cardboard toilet paper tube, and cut them out. Place glow sticks inside the tube, and set your ghostly eyes in a sneaky-but-visible spot near your doorstep—in a bush or potted plant beside the front door.

Hobgoblin Punch Put a little fright into your Halloween party with this clever punch-bowl gag. Pour green Kool-Aid into a latex or rubber glove, tie it closed, then place it in your punch bowl. The floating goblin hand is sure to give your guests the willies.

Frankenstein Fingers These string-cheese Frankenstein fingers are healthy *and* totally creepy. Serve them at a Halloween party or sneak them inside your kids' lunches for a little scare. First, take the string cheese and make the knuckles by cutting slits in the cheese where the knuckles should be. Cut small rectangles out of a green pepper and press them into the tips of the cheese strips to form the monster's fingernails. If needed, add a little cream cheese as an adhesive to keep the nails in place. Spooky!

••

Estimate Your Trick-or-Treater Turnout If you've ever stood in the Halloween candy aisle asking yourself, "How many bags should I buy?" you'll love this tip. As you refill your candy bowl this Halloween, keep track of how many empty bags you've got at the end of the night. Record this number somewhere safe, such as on your computer or smartphone calendar. (You can even set a pop-up reminder for next year's Halloween.) That way, you'll know approximately how much candy to buy ahead of time!

••

Save on Last-Minute Candy Runs If Halloween is coming up and you still haven't picked up your candy, don't worry! (There will *never* be a candy shortage in America.) The timing might be just right for discounts: Wait until the day before for eleventh-hour flash sales.

••

Scare Up Some Face Paint Skip the store-bought face paint this year (along with those yucky chemicals) and make your own nontoxic paints! All you'll need are a few common household items and food coloring: Combine 5 tablespoons cornstarch, 2 tablespoons shortening, 1 tablespoon flour, and a drop of petroleum jelly. Split this mixture into several different containers and add the food dyes as you need them.

Who Knew? Reader's Tip

Nothing says Halloween like chainsaw-inflicted gashes and lots of zombie fluids. Cook up your own fake blood this year by mixing cornstarch, red and blue food dye, and a little milk. Use a small paint-brush to work your bloody magic on faces, necks, limbs, and clothing. —*Blake Gruesser, via Facebook*

Face Paint Remover Face paint is an important part of our kids' Halloween fun. But getting it off easily can be a problem. One trick that's worked for us is olive oil: Simply rub it onto the skin with a dry cloth, then wipe off with a wet cloth.

Turkey-Day Tips

Fun Thanksgiving Activity Give hyper kids something to do *and* decorate your table at the same time this Thanksgiving by sending them out into the yard to find the last remaining yellow, red, and orange leaves. Make sure they're not visibly dirty, then arrange them along the middle of the table in lieu of a runner. We love this activity because it's good for kids of any age, and the older ones can help the younger ones.

Festive Fall Decoration We love this festive-for-fall decoration: Cut a slice off the side of an apple so it lies flat on a saucer or candleholder. Then cut a hole out of the top, and you have an instant votive or tea-light holder! Coat the hole with some lemon juice to keep it from turning brown.

Reuse Corn Decor Are your colorful cobs of Indian corn missing lots of kernels already? Switch it up! Instead of hanging them on the wall, scrape off the rest of the kernels and pour them into a pretty candleholder, small vase, or Mason jar.

Original Pumpkin Project Here's a fun pumpkin project than can be done any time during the fall (even post-Halloween). Get a few small pumpkins and paste fall leaves onto their sides with simple white glue. This is a great craft for after a leaf-gathering expedition—just make sure the leaves are dry before using.

Turkey-Day Stains Be Gone! Prepping for Thanksgiving dinner can be an enormously stressful task—and that's not even counting cleanup time. Here's a great preventative measure we've picked up over the years that helps with our post-meal cleaning: Spray starch your tablecloth a day or two before T-Day, and let it dry for at least a full day. Drips and spills will be no match for your stain-guarded table!

Who Knew? Reader's Tip

Sometimes saving at the store is all about knowing when to shop. Do your Thanksgiving food shopping on the Monday before the holiday, and you'll save a bundle. Stores will be evaluating their holiday stock and will offer discounts on items of which they have excess quantities.

—*Kimberly Monroe, via Facebook*

Cleaner Carving If you've just made a super-juicy roast chicken or turkey, you can congratulate yourself as a cook. But what to do about all of the juices making a mess of your counter as you carve it? Place your cutting board inside a rimmed baking sheet before you cut, and you'll not only have an easy cleanup, you'll also have rich drippings you can use in gravy or broth.

Quick Turkey Fix Did the star of your Thanksgiving dinner come out too dry? Don't panic! You can re-hydrate your meat with an easy braise: Slice up the turkey and stick it in a baking dish. Fill the dish halfway with chicken stock, top with foil, and place it back in the oven for 10 minutes at 350°. The turkey will be juicy and delicious.

Who Knew? Reader's Tip

Your turkey's ready to eat? Move it safely and easily from the pan to the platter by inserting a long wooden spoon into its top and tail (the ends), then lifting carefully.

—*Linda Ann Perlman, via Facebook*

Save a Soupy Stuffing Without question one of the main attractions at our Thanksgiving table, stuffing is hearty, creamy, and comforting—perfect for this family-centric holiday. However, we've had our share of stuffing mishaps; sometimes it's too goopy and wet to eat. To bring soupy stuffing back to life, first spread it onto a baking sheet. Layer cubes of stale bread or unseasoned croutons on top of the stuffing. Pop it back into the oven for about 15 minutes at 375°; when finished, stir it all together and spoon into a serving dish. The bread will sop up excess liquid, leaving your stuffing in its intended scrumptious form.

Find Black Friday Deals The day after Thanksgiving is Black Friday—the craziest shopping day of the year. Before you head out to the mall, hit up FatWallet.com first. They keep track of each store's Black Friday deals, so you can keep an eye out for promised bargains and make a plan of attack for your day of shopping.

Cure Christmas Mayhem

Revamp Your Ribbon Stash If spools of ribbon are overtaking your craft-supply area, give this clever tip a try: Reuse a pants hanger as a ribbon organizer! Place the spools along the rungs of the hanger, then hang in a closet for efficient off-the-floor storage.

Christmas Tree Fresh Test Opting for a beautiful live tree this year? If you're getting a pre-cut tree, make sure you test its freshness before you buy it—you never know how long it's been sitting in the lot exposed to the elements. Try these quick tests to find the freshest tree possible. The Branch Test: Grab a branch firmly between your fingers and gently pull it toward you, then let it go. If lots of needles shake off the tree, it's not fresh enough; if only a few needles fall, the tree is probably still in decent shape. The Fragrance Test: Snap a needle in your fingers and give it a good whiff—the needle should be moist and deliciously pine-scented. If you don't get a pungent dose of pine, the tree is likely drying out.

First Feeding for the Tree Just got your tree up? Great job! Next up: The first feeding. Water your tree with hot water—the temp should be around 80°—then add 2 ounces antibacterial mouthwash. Hot water helps the tree start absorbing water efficiently, and the mouthwash keeps bacteria and mold at bay.

Humidifier for a Healthy Tree The heating system in your home can dry out your tree, dulling its color and piney fresh scent. To give your tree a healthy boost of moisture, place a humidifier in the room to counteract the drying heat—it'll stay fresh, and you can soak up the holiday spirit as long as possible.

Save on Your Tree Skirt Don't waste your money on an expensive tree skirt this Christmas. Instead, look for a small, round tablecloth from a department store—they usually have a big selection and they're inexpensive, too. Cut a round opening in the center for the tree stand, and a straight line to one edge. Place the opening in the back of the tree and you're done.

Baby-Proofing Your Tree If your baby is mobile and curious, as those little ones tend to be, be sure to keep the kid and your Christmas tree safe from tiny roaming hands. Use wire to secure the tree to the wall, ceiling, or any nearby railing or banister. And pick up some large bells from a craft store to add to your tree decorations—any pulling or grabbing will shake the bells, alerting you to baby monkey business.

Prevent a Christmas Cat-astrophe Cat lovers, beware! When it's time to trim the tree, never use tinsel if you have a pet kitty. Cats love to play with tinsel and eat it, and it can be deadly if it gets stuck in their digestive system.

Make It a Safe Christmas for Pets Does your doggie like to lap up the water intended for your Christmas tree? This can be dangerous, thanks to the chemicals lingering in the tree stand. To prevent pets from sneakily re-hydrating at the Christmas tree, wrap the water container in aluminum foil until it reaches several inches up the trunk of your tree. Place your tree skirt over the foil so it isn't visible. When it's time for a refill, simply remove the foil at the top, pour in fresh water, then cover again.

Who Knew? Reader's Tip

Keep your cats from batting ornaments off the tree this Christmas by using this nifty kitty repellent: dryer sheets! Just stick a few underneath your tree skirt, and your furry felines will steer clear of your beautiful tree.   —*Serena Mazotti, via Facebook*

Sappy Hands? We don't like our Christmases to be too sappy—at least, on our hands! One of the easiest ways to remove sticky Christmas tree sap from skin is to rub butter or margarine into the spots. Then sap will come right off, then you can wash your hands as usual with soap and water.

Sap Spill Solution A real Christmas tree adds a deliciously fragrant touch to holiday festivities. Unfortunately, it can also be messy. To combat sap stains on carpets, pour rubbing alcohol onto a cloth and pat it over the sappy spots. The alcohol will de-stick the sap; then you can wipe it away with a clean cloth.

Who Knew? Reader's Tip

If you've ever tried vacuuming up your Christmas tree's pine needles, you know that you end up with a serious clogging problem. To prevent this, simply slip a pantyhose leg over the nozzle, then turn on your vacuum and start cleaning, holding the hose securely in place. The vacuum will suck up the pantyhose along with the needles, creating a sack you can remove once the house is clean.

—*Judy Miller, via Facebook*

The Windup on Christmas Lights When you take down your Christmas tree, always wrap the lights around the outside of a cardboard tube (try the tube from a roll of paper towels) and secure with masking tape. They'll be easy to unwind next year, and you'll never have another nightmarish day of untangling all the lights while the kids wait to decorate the tree.

Safe Storage for Holiday Decorations When it's time to bring down your Christmas tree, take great care with the more delicate ornaments. Slip them into old socks or nylons; then, for extra safety, place them in disposable plastic cups before storing. Old egg cartons are another ultra-safe (and eco-friendly) way to store bulbs and glass trinkets.

Who Knew? Reader's Tip

Have an old hamper you no longer need? Repurpose it as a place to store gift wrap! Rolls of wrapping paper fit perfectly inside, and you can hang door hooks over the edges for rolls of ribbon and gift bags.   —*Kristi Brathwaite, via Twitter*

What to Do with Dusty Decor Save your family from the dust-inflicted sneezies by airing out your stored holiday decorations before you put them up. Place dusty stockings and ornaments in the freezer for a few hours to kill off even more allergens!

Stop Christmas Day Chaos Before It Starts Here's an easy way for your kids to tell which presents belong to whom on Christmas morning: Wrap each child's gifts with his or her own wrapping paper. This is especially helpful if your children aren't able to read gift tags yet. The wrap-

GIFT-WRAPPING TIPS

Frugal Wrapping Paper Use pages from the past year's calendar (photo-side up, obviously) to wrap smaller gifts—two taped together are great for books or DVD sets at Christmastime.

Use Paper Napkins Do you have collections of paper napkins that feel "too pretty to use"? Then use them in a way that takes advantage of their design—as wrapping paper for little gifts or candy bars.

Iron Old Tissue Paper Give used, wrinkled tissue paper a smooth second life this Christmas: Just iron it on the lowest setting and it'll look like new!

Easily De-Wrinkle Your Bows Is your bow and ribbon stash smashed and wrinkled from last year? Stick them in the dryer on low heat along with a dampened cloth and run it for two minutes. The heat plus the moisture from the cloth will pump them back to life.

Gift Wrap Wrapper Prevent leftover wrapping paper from getting dirty, frayed, or ripped at the edges while still on the roll. Cut a lengthwise slit in an empty wrapping paper tube, and wrap it around the roll of paper you'd like to protect. You can leave the very end of the paper sticking out of the cardboard wrapper to create a dispenser.

ping paper tornado will be a little less chaotic if all revelers can spot the presents meant for them from the get-go.

Good-bye, Packing Peanuts Sending presents to friends and family far away? Say "no" to Styrofoam popcorn! Several alternatives are probably already sitting around your home to use—cut-up egg cartons or bunched-up plastic grocery bags. Or, make homemade air pillows with Ziploc bags. Seal them all the way, then open them up just enough to fit a straw through. Blow through the straw to inflate them, then reseal and pack with delicate items.

Eco-Friendly Tree Disposal When Christmas is over and you're finally ready to admit it, consider recycling your tree rather than tossing it in the trash. Search.Earth911.com will help you find recycling centers in your area—they'll shred your trees into reusable mulch, compost, and wood chips, and many offer drop-off and pick-up options.

Keep Your Tree Luscious with LED Lights If it's time for new tree lights, choose mini LED lights over the traditional kind. Not only do they save energy (and cut the cost of electricity), they're also not as hot, preventing your tree from drying out quickly.

Christmas Decorations

Invent Your Own Advent Calendar Let the Christmas countdown begin! Our kids love making their own Advent calendars in anticipation of their number-one favorite holiday of the year. The best part? The "calendar" can be made from anything as long as there are 25 ways to mark off the days until December 25. Here's an easy version to help kick your holiday season into gear: Fasten a clothesline or strand of ribbon to a wall, and attach 25 clothespins. Pin 25 little containers or bags to the clothesline—try small envelopes, cloth sacks, or mini stockings—then slip a little present inside each one. Your kids open one tiny gift per day as yuletide festivities get nearer and nearer.

Advent with Books Count down the days till Christmas with this fun family activity: Pull together all your holiday-themed books and wrap them as individual gifts. Display under the tree or on a shelf. Let your children open one gift per night and read the book together; save "The Night Before Christmas" for the 24th. The pre-holiday festivities might keep your kids satiated enough to lay off the presents under the tree until Christmas!

Easy Christmas Decorating Put those unused holiday ornaments to good use by using them for an inexpensive centerpiece. Simply pick your favorites and put them in a clear punch bowl, and add tinsel or pine sprigs around the base. It works great with those solid-color orbs we always seem to have so many of!

Who Knew? Reader's Tip

For an easy, fun holiday decoration, tie shiny Christmas-colored ribbon around your living room throw pillows—try red, green, white, silver, or gold. You can wrap it around the pillow twice, like you would wrap a gift, and tie a big festive bow on the front.

—*Sarah Thompson Summers, via WhoKnewTips.com*

Clementine Candles for the Holidays Wintertime means clementine season. Rejoice! Not only are they yummy, but clementine peels also make beautiful glowing-from-within candles. Here's how to make your own: With a knife, lightly slice around the circumference of the clementine, only deep enough to cut through the skin. Carefully peel off the skin in two halves without tearing. Set the fruit aside (or eat it). One peel half will have a pith "wick" sticking up from the center; fill about ¼ full with olive oil.

Turn the other peel half facedown on your work surface, and gently slice a shape out of its center—a circle, square, or star shape will do. This is the top of your candle. Use a match to light the oil-soaked wick, and cover with the cutout candle top.

Frost Your Windows If you want your windows to look like they've been touched with frost this holiday season, just mix 1 tablespoon Epsom salts with 1 cup beer, then brush onto the window with a small paintbrush. When you're ready to remove the frost, just wash it off with ammonia and water.

Christmas Window Paint The kids will have fun with this one: Decorate your windows with Christmas greetings and drawings using toothpaste! Not only will the bright-white markings look beautiful from the outside, but once the holiday is over, the toothpaste will also serve as a fantastic window cleaner.

Make Your Home a Winter Wonderland Got any spare cupcake liners on hand? Use them to make pretty paper snowflakes for your living room decorations: Set the liners on a flat surface and press to flatten them. Fold each liner in half, and fold in half again. Using scissors, cut shapes into the folds to create your snowflakes. String them all onto one piece of ribbon or yarn to form a garland, or hang them around the room individually for a beautiful snowy scene.

Who Knew? Reader's Tip

Making a wreath this Christmas with a foam form? Before you begin, slice the foam in half from top to bottom, so that you have two foam circles, each with one rounded side and one flat side. Not only will your wreath hang flat against the door, but now you can make *two*—one wreath for outside and another for inside!
—*Michelle Griffith, via Facebook*

Clean a Wreath with Salt You can easily dust your Christmas wreath by using salt. Go outside in the backyard with a large paper grocery bag and half a cup of salt. Pour the salt in the bag, place the wreath inside, and fold the bag closed. Then shake gently for 20 seconds and your wreath will look as good as new.

Long-Lasting Wreaths We love the look of pine wreaths and garlands, but hate it when needles get all over the floor. To keep the needles from falling, spritz your holiday greenery with hair spray right after you purchase it. The hair spray will keep the needles moist and where they belong.

Deck the Halls—and the Wreath If you're getting tired of that old, drab-looking Christmas wreath, don't get rid of it—just spruce it up a little. Use a glue gun to attach some pinecones from your yard onto it, or buy some cheap doodads at your local crafts store and do the same. You'll get a brand-new wreath for a fraction of the cost, and you won't have to throw out a treasured family decoration.

Who Knew? Reader's Tip

Here's an easy way to hang a wreath on your door: Grab one self-adhesive wall hook—the 3M brand is perfect—and hang it upside down on the reverse side of your door. Loop the wreath's hanging ribbon around the hook, then pull it over the top to the front of the door (where the wreath will hang) for an over-the-door setup. The wreath should hang securely on the front.

—*Jennifer Boudinot, via Facebook*

Outdoor Christmas Decorations When pruning your trees and bushes in the spring or summer, make sure to save some branches for later use. Then spray paint them red, white, silver, or gold and you have an instant Christmas decoration! Place them in planters of flowers that are dead for the winter, and add lights or ornaments for extra flair.

Christmas Traditions

Santa's Recycling System We love this "toy recycling" idea so much that it's become a favorite tradition in our home. When the kids make their wish lists, they should also decide which old toys they'd like to give back to Santa for Christmastime recycling—Santa and his elves refurbish the old toys so he can give them to less fortunate children. If your kids are older, bring the toys to the Goodwill or Salvation Army together. Not only does this help de-clutter the house, it also inspires heartwarming Christmas spirit in little kids and big ones alike.

Frugal Christmas? If opening presents is going to take drastically less time than usual this year, fill the gap by starting some new Christmas traditions. Make a popcorn string for the tree, cut out sugar cookies with different-colored sugars for decoration, or try this game to make gift-opening take longer (it's a favorite at our gatherings):

Find as many holiday present rejects as you have people playing—candles with bad scents, weird gifts from coworkers, or silly finds from the dollar store. Wrap each one and have each guest pick a gift. Go around the room clockwise, starting with the youngest person. Before opening their gift, guests can decide to trade with someone else (even if that person's gift has been unwrapped). After one round of gift opening, have one more round of trades, with players deciding if they want to keep their current gift or switch with someone else. You'll be surprised which gifts people actually like, and get a laugh at the worst one.

DIY Christmas Poppers Christmas poppers are a British tradition and have found their way into many American homes. You can make your own at home by loading a toilet paper tube with candy and little toys, then using wrapping paper to cover the tube completely, leaving extra paper on each end. Tie the ends with ribbon, then let kids yank them open from the sides to reveal their prizes!

Make Gift-Guessing Harder We like to add a little more excitement and surprise to the holidays by labeling our kids' gifts with colorful stickers rather than gift tags. The stickers are color-coded for each recipient, and we don't reveal the code until gift-opening time on Christmas Day.

The Mall and Beyond: Savvy Shopping Tips

At-the-Store Know-How

Saving on Clothes, Accessories,
and More

Car-Buying Secrets

Getting the Best Deals on
Big-Ticket Items

At-the-Store Know-How

Know What You're Getting Before you're convinced
to buy something just because it's on sale, make sure to
carefully consider the discount offer. For example, when
something is offered for 25 percent off, with an additional
25 percent taken at the register, you're usually not actually getting 50 percent off—you're getting 25 percent of
25 percent—or 43.75 percent off. Also, make sure to ask
whether "buy one, get one free" promotions require you
to purchase two items, or if you can simply get one for 50
percent off. Finally, be aware that many stores put quan-
tity limits on sale items just to try to convince consumers
that the product is in demand. Buying more than you regularly would doesn't save you money—it makes them more.

Take Your Time Big stores are experts at eye-catching
displays that grab your attention—and pull it away from
something else. When hunting for deals, make sure to
look through your other options (especially those on the
bottom shelves) to see if there is a better price to be had
away from the bright colors and flashing lights. Don't let
the cash register be the first place you see all of your
purchases in front of you—grab a spot on the floor or an
empty desk in the furniture section and lay out everything
you plan on buying before you head up to the front. You'll

HAGGLING HINTS

Do Your Research Before you go to the store, do a little research at competing stores or on the internet beforehand. If you ask a salesperson to match the price at a nearby store, there's a good chance he or she will.

Be Nice Remember that haggling shouldn't be aggressive. Start by simply asking "Is there any flexibility in the price?" and see what kind of answer you get.

Cost-Cutting Cops One of the best methods for negotiating at the store is the "good cop, bad cop" strategy, so make sure to bring your spouse or a friend. One of you acts really interested in the product, while the other continually points out the flaws and negative aspects. Because of the "good cop," the salesperson will remain hopeful that he can sell the product, but "bad cop" will make him work for it.

Ask Everywhere Did you know that, with sales slipping, the staffs of chain stores like Home Depot and Best Buy are now being told that bargaining is OK? Make sure you don't tell yourself "this place won't lower the price just because I ask."

Accessories Lead to Discounts If you're buying a big-ticket item and several accessories for it, make sure to ask for a discount on your purchase. Most stores have a higher mark-up on accessories for top-selling items so that they can sell the main attraction at a discount.

have more time to consider your purchases than when they're about to be scanned.

Return to the Scene for Even More Deals You're shopping in your favorite store and notice that there are tons of markdowns. After you fill your arms with bargains, go home and mark the day on your calendar! Most stores receive shipments of new goods every 9–12 weeks and discount current merchandise to make room for the new stuff. Return to the store during that time frame to find more deals.

Avoid Impulse Purchases If you're someone who is susceptible to making a lot of impulse purchases, make sure you have a clear head when thinking about what to buy. Take a seat by the bathrooms and play a quick game on your cell phone or people-watch for a few minutes. Once you've had a little while to relax, you may look at what you're about to buy in a different light.

Use Your Phone to Check Prices If you're lucky enough to own an iPhone, Android, or other smartphone, you're also lucky to have access to applications that make shopping easier. Once the app is installed, you can use your phone's camera to take a snapshot of the barcode, or enter the UPC numbers underneath. Your phone will then give you a list of how much the item costs at locations near you and online. Search your phone's app store for Barcode Scanner on iPhone and Android, ScanLife on Blackberry, and ShopSavvy for Windows phones. If you don't have a smartphone, you can still easily compare prices online. You don't get to use your phone as a scanner (which is half the fun), but you can enter the UPC code of any product to get prices from around the web by using Google's Product Search (Products.Google.com). Just type in the numbers found near the barcode and away you go!

See Also . . . For secrets on how to save while shopping online, check out the Internet Secrets: Saving and Earning Online chapter!

Saving on Clothes, Accessories, and More

Keep It Simple When you're buying clothes, always go for classic looks rather than modern, trendy ones. A blue V-neck T-shirt will be fashionable year after year, while something with more exotic colors or patterns will go out of style quickly. By choosing the basics, you won't have to buy as many new articles of clothing each season.

Begin in the (Bargain) Basement How many times have you purchased an $80 sweater, only to find a nearly identical one for much less later? When you begin to look for clothes for the new season, always start at the least expensive store first. Since most clothing stores carry similar items each season, you'll make sure to get each piece for the best price. You should also try to buy most of your basics—solid-color T-shirts, socks, and so forth—at the cheaper stores. Save the expensive stores for the uniquely designed and patterned clothes, where you can see the difference in quality.

Who Knew? Reader's Tip

If you are in one of those warehouse stores where you can't try on clothes, but you want to see if a shirt will be the right size, try this tip: Fold the shirt down at the point under the sleeves. You can then hold it across your chest and see if it matches up to the seams on the shirt you are wearing. —*C. M. Drybrae, via email*

The Seasonal Shopping Secret For the best deals on clothes, shop in the off-season. Buy spring and summer clothing in July and August, and fall and winter clothing in January and February. (You can often find the best sales right after the holiday season.) It's sometimes a bummer to buy something you're not going to be able to wear for six months, but when the time comes to switch seasons, you'll be happy you already have some new clothes to wear—all of which were purchased on sale!

Take It to the Tailor Going to a tailor may seem like an expensive proposition, but it's often worth it if you unearth a good deal on a suit or other item of clothing that doesn't quite fit. Found some jeans for 10 bucks that look great but are an inch too long? A jacket that's a steal, but a bit too baggy in the arms? For a small price, you can get these items custom-fitted at a tailor. And you'll still be saving a bundle from what the normal retail price would be.

Who Knew? Reader's Tip

When you buy a new bath towel set, purchase an extra washcloth, because the washcloths are always the first part of the set to wear out. That way, you can get more use out of the more-expensive bath and hand towels.   —*Ruth Niersbach, via email*

Ask and You Shall Receive Believe it or not, many stores—especially department stores—have coupons available just for the asking. You may not see them advertised in the store, but if you go up to the customer service counter and ask for any current coupons, don't be surprised if you're handed some big savings!

When Junk Mail Is Good The best and easiest way to get coupons to most stores is to make sure you're on their mailing list—both email and "real" mail. Though you may not like the idea of signing yourself up for junk mail, you'll also be surprised at the number of coupons you'll receive simply because the store knows you want them. Visit your favorite stores' websites to sign up for their email mailing list; you may need to visit their customer service counter in the store to see if you can sign up for a mailing list to receive physical coupons in the mail. Many stores also have a loyalty program. Ask and see what's available!

Hit the Web Before Hitting the Mall Did you know that the websites of many malls now offer coupons? If you're headed to the mall, check their site for exclusive coupons and links to the coupons offered by the websites of the various stores inside.

Pick Your Color Not happy with the color of a handbag or pair of fancy shoes? Instead of buying new accessories, turn that unbecoming chartreuse into an elegant black with a can of shoe color spray. You can pick up an inexpensive can of shoe color from a repair shop, then revamp those heels yourself instead of paying someone else to do it for you.

．．

Discounts on Glasses If you need new glasses and aren't sure how you're going to afford them, check out 39DollarGlasses.com. For around $45 (with shipping), you can get attractive (though bare-bones) glasses, including the lenses! Walmart also offers good deals on frames and lenses. If you're looking for something more stylish, try WarbyParker.com, which offers fantastic prices on frames that look brand name. Plus, you can try out their glasses online "virtually" by uploading a picture of yourself. Neat!

．．

Contact Lenses If you have a prescription for contacts, you can get a certificate for a free pair of Acuvue disposable lenses at Acuvue.com. Just click on the "Free trial lenses" link.

．．

See Also . . . For more ideas on how to get coupons, head to the Grocery Store Savings chapter!

．．

Car-Buying Secrets

Take the Stress Out of Car Buying The next time you are looking to buy a car, visit CarWoo.com. You enter the make, model, and options you're looking for, and a network of local car dealers will bid for your business. You aren't hassled by phone calls from the dealerships, so you can shop on your own schedule and negotiate with the dealers anonymously. It's a great way to buy a new or used car!

Who Knew? Reader's Tip

If you're buying a new car and can't afford a hybrid, consider going with a stick shift rather than an automatic. Not only are manual cars often cheaper, manually changing gears saves energy because your car is using only as much energy as it needs to—it's never in a higher gear than it should be. Being able to coast down hills also saves you tons. —*Joe Martinez, via Facebook*

Great Tip for Test Drives If you're buying a car, make sure you test-drive it at night. Driving in the dark will give you an opportunity to make sure the car's lights work and will draw your attention inward toward its dash, so that you take in all of its interior features and can decide whether or not you like them.

. . . .

Best Car Advice After gas, one of the biggest costs associated with having a car is the interest you pay on the loan. Before you go buy a car, get a loan in place first—the financing the car dealership will offer most likely won't be as competitive. Know your credit rating, and check with your employer's credit union or look online for deals on car loans. A good place to begin is a page that lets you compare rates and find out information on car loans. One site we like is BankRate.com. Click on "Auto" from the homepage.

Getting the Best Deals on Big-Ticket Items

. . . .

Know When to Buy Did you know that you can score big savings just by knowing what days of the week online retailers tend to discount their goods? Monday is the best day to buy computers and other electronics—retailers want to get your attention at the beginning of the workweek, and they offer sales on cameras, personal computers, and other items. They also try to create excitement about TVs during the first half of the week so that they'll score weeklong sales, so buy a TV on Monday, Tuesday, or Wednesday. Sunday is the best day to buy appliances. Most people buy appliances on Fridays and Saturdays, and if sales aren't going well, some stores may mark down appliances even further.

Who Knew? Reader's Tip

Looking for coupons for big-ticket items for your home like washing machines, TVs, and more? Stop by your local post office and grab a packet for people who are moving and would like their mail forwarded. Even if you don't fill out the forwarding card, these packets often contain coupons from stores targeting those who have recently moved.

—*Marybeth Gauthier, via Facebook*

Re: Rebates Have you ever bought an expensive item and wondered if there's a manufacturer's rebate out there you don't know about? For a list of thousands of rebates on all types of items, head to PriceGrabber.com/home_rebates .php. This fantastic site gives you everything you need to take advantage of all the rebates currently being offered, including links to the rebate form online. Best of all, you can easily sort them by item type and/or its brand name.

Rah-Rah for Refurbs If you're like most people, you probably shy away from buying refurbished electronics, but you shouldn't. We go out of our way to buy refurbs, which not only save cash, but also provide more or less the same level of reliability as brand-new items. Whether it's a cell phone, laptop, gaming console, or television, a refurbished item is arguably less likely to be defective than a new one, because these items are tested at the factory before they're resold. And in the rare instance where a refurb does fail, all of the other refurbs you've bought will have saved you enough money to replace it. Contrary to popular opinion, most refurbished units aren't simply broken items that have been repaired. They may have been returned to the maker for any number of other reasons. A customer may have returned a gift he didn't want, the packaging (but not the actual item) may have been damaged in shipping, the item might have a cosmetic blemish, or the item may have been missing a nonessential accessory. If you can live with those things, then refurbished items are definitely for you. Many of them even come with the original manufacturer's warranty intact.

Get Free Tech Support It turns out that membership to Sam's Club gives you a lot more than bargain prices! Even if you didn't buy your computer, TV, or other electronic from Sam's Club, you can still call their 24-hour tech support for help at 877-758-4346. Costco will also help

PHONE-BUYING SECRETS

Where to Buy a Mobile Phone The most expensive place to buy a cell phone is at a cell phone store, even one run by your mobile provider. These stores count on foot traffic and impulse purchases, and usually price phones higher. When it's time to get a new phone, check out your phone company's online offerings, which will include several free or heavily discounted phones that the stores no longer carry.

Consider Pay-as-You-Go If you find yourself vastly under-using your mobile minutes each month, consider canceling your current plan when your contract runs out and paying as you go instead. Some now have smartphone features, and they can save you tons.

When Insurance Is a Bad Idea When purchasing a cell phone, never sign up for insurance or a warranty. The cost of taking your chances and buying a cheap replacement if necessary is much less than paying a fee each month for insurance.

The Best Things Come . . . If you don't care about having the latest model of cell phone, wait until the latest model comes out—and then buy last year's model. With the new release, you'll see heavy discounts in the older phones.

members with tech problems, as long as the item was purchased at their store. Give them a call at 866-861-0450.

. . . .

Furniture-Finding Facts It's nice to be able to look at furniture in person before you buy it, but the internet usually has the cheapest prices. The solution? While you're at the store, write down the piece of furniture's brand and model number (which can usually be found on the price tag). Then type that information into Google and see what prices come up.

Who Knew? Reader's Tip

Looking for inexpensive, quality building supplies? Check out one of Habitat for Humanity's ReStores, which sell used and surplus wood and other building materials for low prices. To find a location nearest you, visit Habitat.org/env/restores.
—*Deb Bouman, via Facebook*

Color Matching If you're shopping for accessories to match a color on a bedspread, couch, or piece of art, taking a photo often doesn't cut it. Especially if you print it out on your home printer, the variance in color from the photograph to the actual article can be dramatic. Instead, go to a paint store and pick up paint swatches that you think are similar in shade. Then go home and find the closest match. Mark that color, then bring the swatch to the store instead.

. . . .

Spring for New Furniture If a new living room set is in your plans, start shopping in March. Furniture retailers debut new designs each spring, so older items are on sale then.

. . . .

Best Time to Buy Big If you're looking to buy large appliances or household furnishings like a washing machine, dryer, dishwasher, refrigerator, or sofa, the best time to buy is in October. At this time of year, businesses are busy making room for their holiday inventory, so you'll find tons of sales on last year's merchandise. Go ahead, celebrate a little early!

. . . .

Just Say "No" to Store Cards When offered financing by a store you are purchasing a big-ticket item from, think carefully before you accept. If they basically give you a store credit card with a spending limit that matches the price of the item, this credit card will pop up on your credit report as being opened and immediately maxed out. Obviously, this isn't good news for your credit score.

. . . .

Cash for Trash Most major appliances, like refrigerators, freezers, dishwashers, washers, and dryers should last

10–15 years. When it's time to replace them, though, don't just throw them out! Recyclers like Jaco Environmental will may pay you for old appliances. Visit their website at JacoInc.net to search by zip code and find out whether your local utility company is offering a cash-back offer.

Fridge Facts Labels can be misleading when looking for the right sized refrigerator, because they're measured in cubic feet—and that includes space taken up by the freezer, ice maker, and shelves. Here's a good rule of thumb to help you figure it out: For a family of four, look for 18–20 cubic feet, including 5 cubic feet for the freezer.

Keep Cold Appliances Cold It may be time to rearrange your kitchen for energy-efficient savings. Keeping appliances that heat things up (like a stove, oven, or toaster) away from your refrigerator will make it easier for your fridge and freezer to stay cold, saving you lots of money.

TV Time In the market for a new flat screen? If you miss the great deals that are usually offered on Black Friday, wait until February. That's right after the International Consumers Electronic Show is held, where major retailers see new items that will be delivered in March. You'll find some terrific bargains right before the new TVs come to market!

chapter 8

Internet Secrets for Saving and Making Money

· ·

Our Favorite Sites for Savings

Saving in the Golden Years If you're a senior, you already know that you're entitled to great discounts at the movies, restaurants, museums, and other spots. To make sure you're getting every discount, visit Sciddy.com. Enter your zip code, and you'll find local deals for restaurants, medical care, entertainment, home repairs, and more! There may be some local deals you never knew existed. Who doesn't love senior discounts?

Your Own Personal Shopper At ShopItToMe.com, you enter your favorite brands of clothes and your sizes and they do all the online searching for you. When items come up for sale on a department store's site, they'll send you an email, alerting you to the discount. The best part is, you can specify your size, so you won't have to waste your time wading through links only to find that the store is all out of extra-large!

In a Flash In the last few years, the number of flash sale websites has increased dramatically. If you're not familiar with them, these sites offer designer merchandise at drastically reduced prices. The sales usually start around 11 a.m. Eastern time, and there are two catches: Items sell out fast, and returns are not usually permitted. If you take the plunge, though, they can be a great way of scoring everything from fab children's clothing and high-end home decor to designer handbags and snazzy stilettos. Some of our favorites are OneKingsLane.com and JossAndMain.com for home furnishings, Ideeli.com for women's fashion and accessories, and TheMiniSocial.com for kids' clothing, toys, and decor.

For Refurbished Finds You may have heard that buying refurbished products is a great way to save because they've had a once-over by their original manufacturers and still have warranties in place. One of the best places we've found to score major discounts on refurbished appliances, electronics, tools, patio furniture, mattresses, and more is SearsOutlet.com. They sell refurbished, lightly dented or scratched, and returned items. For example, you can save 75 percent on a reconditioned refrigerator and around 60 percent on a dryer. And the new product warranties apply! The only downside is that the shipping can get pricey, although many items can be shipped to a nearby Sears store for free.

Fast Shoe Deals At Zappos.com, you'll find more shoes than you ever imagined possible, including men's, women's, and kids' sneakers; dress shoes; boots; and sandals.

WEBSITE SAVINGS TRICKS

Online Shopping Hint When you're visiting a company's online store, make sure to hit up the "sale" section first. Many sites will also keep sale items in their original locations—without the prices marked down. Look in the sale section first to make sure you're getting the best price.

Lazy Savings Here's an online shopping tip you'll have to see to believe: When you're shopping online and want to purchase an item, place it in the "Shopping cart" and then leave the site. Many e-retailers will send you an email with a discount code within a day to entice you to buy, so you save big by simply waiting!

Cookie Tip Companies are more likely to offer coupons to new customers in the hopes of enticing them to buy. So before you shop online, try clearing your internet browser's cookies (its Help menu will usually tell you how). You'll be surprised how many coupons pop up when the site thinks you've never been there before.

Zip Up Savings If you're looking for coupons online and are asked your zip code, try typing in a few different zip codes to see what crops up. While the coupon company only wants certain zip codes to access certain coupons, your grocery store doesn't know the difference, and you can still use them!

Not only do they have free shipping, they also include a return shipping label with your order, so if you don't like the shoes once you try them on, you can easily return them for free. Another great site for shoes is 6pm.com, which carries lots of shoes that used to be on Zappos. You do have to pay shipping, but the savings can be worth it because the selection and prices are usually quite good.

Deals on Brands If you're trying to save money, it's probably a good idea to try to stay away from designer fashion labels. But if you just can't help yourself, Bluefly .com is the best place to go for a bargain. You'll find discounted prices on men's and women's designer clothing, including such labels as Kenneth Cole, Burberry, Armani, Marc Jacobs, Calvin Klein, and Prada. Just try to keep it to a couple of outfits and a handbag!

Helpful Websites
You Should Know

Begin the Journey to a Healthier Life Trends in dieting seem to change with the season. One day you're being told to eat plain toast, the next, bacon—it all gets a little confusing! That's where FatSecret.com comes in.

Create a personalized exercise and nutrition program, then share it with their online community for moral support and feedback. Plus, you can track your progress, keep an online fitness journal, and research different diets and fitness techniques. Another fitness site we love is MyHomePersonalTrainer.com, where you can calculate your ideal weight and heart rate, assess your cardiovascular fitness, and receive all sorts of free advice to help you start getting in shape.

To-Do Lists Made Easy We absolutely adore Remember the Milk, a task organizer that goes far beyond your web browser. Even if you don't have a fancy phone, you can add things to your online calendar and get reminders from your cell phone! It also allows you to easily share lists and calendars (like with your spouse), and map your appointments before you go. To find out more and download for free, go to RememberTheMilk.com.

Free Virtual Assistant Here's a great, unique resource for keeping track of shopping and to-do lists, appointments, and important tasks: Record your own reminders using ReQall (Reqall.com), a voice-recognition service that will alert you to daily tasks and due dates that you enter yourself ahead of time. You'll first need to download the program onto your computer or smartphone, then call the toll-free number and leave yourself a reminder! ReQall will also transcribe your voice messages and send them back via email, text, or instant message. Who needs a real-life personal assistant?

Who Knew? Reader's Tip

If you or someone in your family has a food allergy, check out LivingWithout.com. They have recipes, substitutions, and health information for those with gluten, dairy, and other food sensitivities. It's a great help for meal planning and party food ideas.   —*Terry Scargle, via Facebook*

The Best Place for Recipes Our favorite site for free recipes is Epicurious.com, where you can search for recipes by type (appetizers, drinks, entrees, etc.), or type in keywords to search for specific recipes. Since their recipes are pulled from publications like *Bon Appétit* and *Gourmet*, you know they're going to be good, but if you're not sure, you can read reader reviews. You can also start a "recipe box" of your favorite recipes from the site—make sure to include one of their more than 400 recipes for chocolate cake!

Resources for Kids Whether you homeschool your children or one of them has expressed interest in a particular subject, it's hard to know where to turn online for accurate information. At Free.Ed.gov, you can find free, professional learning resources—including online videos, audio lectures, interactive features, and printable lessons—from government agencies. They list information by subject, including math, health, the arts, state history, and more.

Finding Money for College These days, college can cost $10,000–$35,000 for one year! And that's just for a bachelor's degree. The good news is that there is a lot of free money out there, from grants and scholarships to assistantships and fellowships. Here are some ways to find it. FedMoney.org is probably the most comprehensive online resource on all US government grants and student financial aid programs. Here, you will find detailed information about who is eligible and how to apply for more than 130 government grants and loans related to education. You can also check the US Department of Education's site at StudentAid.ed.gov.

Does a Company Owe You Money? Hundreds of lawsuits are settled every day, entitling purchasers of products to money they don't know about. At TopClassActions.com, find easy-to-navigate lists of recent settlements and how to get money from them. During one recent visit, we found out Costco owed us a free three-month membership and anyone with AT&T internet service could get $2.90 for every month they had subscribed!

Savings Bonds You May Not Know About Did you know that more than 25,000 mature savings bonds aren't cashed each year? To find out if there is a bond in your name that you didn't know or have forgotten about, check out TreasuryHunt.gov or call 1-800-722-2678.

Who Knew? Reader's Tip

If you or a deceased family member received service medals from the army, navy, air force, marines, or other service and they have been lost, you can obtain free replacements from the US government. For more information, visit Archives.gov/veterans/replace-medals.html.

—*Lisa Waters Harris, via Facebook*

The 411 on Major Appliances Washing machine just broke down, and you're not sure if it's still under warranty? Need to replace a part in your dishwasher, but don't know what its specifications are? Want to buy a microwave and not sure what you should be looking for? Find the answers at Appliance411.com. They have purchasing information (including rebates), FAQs about appliances big and small, and best yet, online manuals and warranty information for just about any model of any appliance. If you're looking for help with any machine in your home, go here first.

Trees Are Treasure If you've ever wanted to plant a tree in your yard, you were probably taken aback by the large price tag. But did you know that many municipalities offer free trees? Call your town or county's department of public works and see if they have any free tree programs. The next best place for free trees is ArborDay.org. Become a member for only $10 and receive 10 free trees that will grow well where you live, plus discounts on future purchases. Their website is also a fantastic resource for learning how to care for trees and troubleshooting tree problems.

Painting Tool If you've ever painted an entire room and wished you could change the color with a snap of your fingers, then this freebie is for you. Visit Behr.com and register with their site to use their "Paint Your Place" program for free. It will allow you to upload a picture of a room in your home, then change the wall color without having to buy a bucket of paint (and spend all day painting).

Junk Mail Be Gone! Sick of getting a million credit card offers every time you open your mailbox? You can opt out for free by visiting OptOutPrescreen.com (or call 1-888-567-8688). Signing up will eliminate all of those "pre-approved" offers from taking up space in your mailbox and your trashcan. While you're at it, visit DMAChoice.org to remove yourself from even more companies' mailing lists.

Find Free ATMs Sick of paying up to $3 every time you have to visit an ATM? At AllPointNetwork.com, you can find all of the surcharge-free ATMs in your area by entering your city and state or your zip code. Many of the listings are for stores that offer cash back with purchase, but you never know when you'll find a free ATM you never knew about.

Free Accounting Help We know how hard it can be to deal with money stress. But Voyant can help. Visit PlanWithVoyant.com to map your financial goals (such as buying a home, saving for retirement, or paying for your kids' college) along an interactive timeline. It's a great way to plan for the future and chart your progress.

Help Filing Your Taxes The IRS free-filing service provides free federal income tax return preparation and electronic filing for all taxpayers. All you need is access to a computer and the Internet and you can prepare and e-file your federal tax return for free! The service offers two options. The first, called Free File, is for filers whose incomes are $57,000 per year or less. Free File allows you to prepare your taxes using one of the 20 tax preparation software products on their site. If you make more than $57,000, the IRS has decided you can afford to pay for these programs yourself! But you can still use their Free File Fillable Forms, which are electronic versions of the usual paper forms that you can file online for free. To access either service, go to IRS.gov/freefile.

Who Knew? Reader's Tip

If you can never remember your computer passwords, consider trying out RoboForm.com. This neat site keeps track of your passwords on one encrypted site, then enters them when you're at sites that require passwords.

—*Sammi Miller, via Facebook*

An Actually Free Credit Score Did you know that legally, you are entitled to one free credit report per year? However, many credit report sites will make you pay to see your score, or charge you a membership or "credit monitoring" fee. Visit CreditKarma.com for a free, no-strings-attached estimation of your credit score. Then go to AnnualCreditReport.com to see how they came up with that score, and to make sure there are no errors on your report.

Live to Learn At GCFLearnFree.org, you can finally learn how to use all those computer programs that have been befuddling you. Sign up for classes taught over the internet, or download learning materials to go at your own pace. Classes include Microsoft Windows, Word, Excel, internet searching, and email basics. The site also offers free lessons in managing money, math skills, and "everyday life" problems.

Online Computer Help For something called "Help," that particular menu item on any computer program is unbelievably unhelpful! The next time you find yourself throwing your hands up in frustration in front of the computer, head over to ProTonic.com. Type in a question, and get a free, prompt email response from a volunteer computer expert. Who needs an IT department?

Why Pay for Microsoft? "Great software that's easy to use . . . and free!" That's the claim at OpenOffice.org, and it's true. Check out their free word processing and spreadsheet programs that are similar to programs that Microsoft offers. Another good site for these types of programs is

Google Docs: Docs.Google.com. At Google Docs you can open Microsoft Word and other files, then share them over the internet with others.

Who Knew? Reader's Tip

Tons of coffee shops, bookstores, hotels, and public buildings offer wireless internet service for free or free-with-purchase. Find local "hot spots" at WiFiFreeSpot.com, and don't forget to submit any WiFi zones you find for others on the go.

—*Kristen Harrison, via Twitter*

Résumé Resources Get all kinds of free, professional advice on your career (or desired career) in one place: CareerOneStop.com (or call 1-877-348-0502). It will give you tutorials on résumés and cover letters, give you salary information, help you find free classes in your area, and more. If you're working on your résumé, check out ResumeCompanion.com. Indicate what position you're applying for, and it will give you the perfect phrases to describe the type of work you've done at previous employers.

How Do I...? To learn how to do just about anything, visit WonderHowTo.com, which culls instructional videos from more than 1,700 websites. You can check out what's hot, do a custom search, or browse through such categories as family, electronics, software, dance, fitness, magic tricks, and pets. Whether you want to learn how to cut your own hair, use Photoshop software, or make a shot glass out of ice, you'll find it here.

Visit WhoKnewTips.com We don't mind doing a bit of shameless self-promotion for our site, WhoKnewTips.com, because we know you're sure to find some great freebies and money-saving ideas when you visit. In addition to listing the most recent freebies and discounts we've found around the web, we also post our latest tips, updated daily. You can also get our Tip of the Day via Twitter, Facebook, Instagram, and other social media at @whoknewtips.

Making Money Online

Make Money Off Your Style Are your friends always asking you for clothing recommendations? You can set up your own virtual store from thousands of brands they have available at StyleOwner.com. Send people to your store and if they buy something, you get 10 percent! It's a great way to make extra money without having to spend a cent in start-up costs.

The Survey Says . . . The folks at SurveySpot.com not only want your opinion, they'll pay for it. Join for free and you'll receive 5–7 surveys each week to complete. For each completed survey, they'll pay you $2–$10 or enter you in a sweepstakes (or both!). This and other survey sites like MySurvey.com, EPoll.com, and Toluna.com can be frustrating because you don't always qualify to take the survey and it can take a while to earn money, but if you enjoy answering questions and have a bit of free time, this is a great way to earn some extra cash while you're messing around on the web.

Who Knew? Reader's Tip

If you're looking to make a little extra cash talking about products you love, check out Looqiloo.com. You upload a video review of a particular product to the site; it can be anything from cell phones and electronics to personal-care products and books. When users watch the video, they'll see a link to buy the product (often through Amazon); you'll receive a percentage of the sale as a commission.
—*Jackie Talbot, via Facebook*

Cash for Your Gadgets Now you can keep your old electronics out of the landfill and possibly get some free cash in exchange! Services such as BuyMyTronics.com and

Gazelle.com recycle or refurbish your old cast-offs and send you a check in return. Just fill out the easy forms on their websites. They'll make you an offer and, if you accept, send you a box with postage to send your gizmo to them. They take cameras, cell phones, MP3 players, game consoles, personal computers, and more.

Get Money for Ink Cartridges Got empty cartridges for a printer, copier, or fax machine? TonerBuyer.com will buy them from you, and even pay the shipping! Fill out their online form to find out how much your cartridges are worth, then print out the prepaid mailing form and wait for your check in the mail. You can also bring empty printer cartridges into Staples stores, which will get you a $2 credit (up to 10 a month).

Rent What You Own If you have a household item you rarely use (or need extra cash fast), how about renting it? Zilok.com allows you to rent out your car, vacation home, tools, camera, lawn mower, TV, video game console, and more. (Unfortunately, you can't rent out your kids.) For more information, go to US.Zilok.com/support.

What to Do with Unwanted Gift Cards Has that gift card to Smitty's Bird Bath Emporium that your aunt gave you been sitting on your desk for years? Head over to

PlasticJungle.com or GiftCardRescue.com to get cash from unused gift cards! They'll pay you a portion of the total cost of your card (around 80 percent–90 percent) and re-sell it on their site. If you've purchased a deal from a site like Groupon or Living Social that you now realize you're not going to use before it expires, check out the site CoupRecoup.com, where you can sell your purchased deals to someone who will use them.

Test Websites for Money Help web developers find out the ways in which their websites are confusing or not working well by becoming a tester for UserTesting.com. They'll give you software to install on your computer that tracks your mouse's movements, and ask you to narrate a short video while you use the site. After answering a few questions, you'll be paid $10 per site you review. To find out more information, visit UserTesting.com/be-a-user-tester.

Easily Sell Handmade Items Are you a crafter? A knit-ter? A genius with papier mâché? Etsy.com will give you a worldwide venue to sell your item. Sign up for free and get your very own virtual shop, then pay 20¢ for every item you list. You can set the price at whatever you want, and when it sells, you pay Etsy 3.5 percent of the price to han-dle the credit card transaction. You can also pay extra fees to be featured on the Etsy home page, which is visited by thousands of people looking to buy handmade items.

....

Share Your Skills Do you have something you teach? Join SkillShare.com and connect with people across America who want to learn your skill, which could be anything from cooking to origami to selling real estate. SkillShare gives you a unique forum to list your class and your price per student, and will even help you find a place to hold your class. In return, it takes 15 percent of the fee you collect. A similar site is Limu.com.

....

Extra Money for Photographers If you have a gift for taking beautiful photographs, there may be a side career for you in photography. Advertise your services to become a wedding and special events photographer, and make some extra dough on the weekends—just make sure you have a sophisticated website where people can view your work. You can also make money selling your images to publishers and creative professionals who are looking for stock photography. Go to Shutterpoint.com, Dreamstime. com, or iStockPhoto.com to find out more about selling your images online.

....

Are You a Quick Typist? Make that typing class you took way back when pay off! If you're quick and accurate when it comes to typing things up on the computer, you may want to try out Workers.VirtualBee.com. Register with the site and take an evaluation test, and you'll be on their list of people willing to type for cash! You'll get paid per 1,000 (accurate) characters/keystrokes, and the amount changes depending on their demand and supply of typists. Workload also varies, but some people have reported getting a lot of work around tax time. In any case, if you're quick at a keyboard it's worth checking out!

Who Knew? Reader's Tip

If you're a good writer and have a love for your local community, why not share your knowledge with others for a little cash? Examiner.com regularly hires writers to write about events and community interest articles from around town. Just go to Examiner.com and click on "Write for us." DemandStudios.com (which supplies articles to eHow.com) also hires writers, as well as copyeditors and videographers. The base pay isn't much, but you'll get more money as you get more hits to your page.   —*Kerri Churchill, via Facebook*

Work from Home for Google Did you know that Google occasionally offers telecommuting jobs? Though open positions are not always easy to come by, it's worth it to check out Google.com/about/jobs/locations/multiple to see if they have any openings. Some jobs, like reading their ads to make sure they make sense, don't have many requisite skills, and you still get to work for one of the top-rated companies in the world!

Who Knew? Reader's Tip

In this day and age, many of the things entrepreneurs sell come in the form of files—whether they're songs, photography, ebooks, designs, or any of the other many things that fill our online world. GumRoad.com makes it ridiculously easy to sell files to friends, family, and anyone who follows you online. Simply upload a file and set your price, and GumRoad gives you a link you can email, tweet, or share on Facebook. To buy, all someone has to do is enter their email and credit card info, and GumRoad sends them an email with a link to your content! Best of all, GumRoad's cut is only 25¢ plus 5 percent, lower than most other sites that allow you to sell products. —*John Roche, via WhoKnewTips.com*

Make oDesk Your Desk If you're looking for a job, you've probably spent plenty of time on online job ads. But oDesk.com is something different. They specialize in hiring freelancers and other work-from-home professionals.

Create a free account and you can browse "help wanted" listings for administrative assistants, bookkeepers, writers, illustrators, salespeople, IT managers, software developers, and much more. Apply and even interview right through their site.

....

Bilingual Benjamins Do you know more than one language well enough to translate written words? If so, you can make between $10 and $50 an hour working from home. Visit TranslatorBase.com to find people needing freelance translators for material in many languages, including English, Spanish, Chinese, French, German, Japanese, Portuguese, Italian, Greek, Russian, Arabic, Korean, and many more. Projects range from large websites to a single marriage document.

....

Get Paid for Your Idea Do you have an idea for a great invention, but not enough money to get it off the ground? Then you'll love Quirky.com. Submit an idea for a new product on the site, and get feedback from the Quirky community on how to make it better. Then put it up for a vote on the site and if your product wins, it will be manufactured and sold to companies like Target, Toys "R" Us, Barnes & Noble, and more—and you'll get a portion of the proceeds! To find out more information, go to Quirky.com/learn.

....

Finding Free Stuff Online

How About a House Party? What could be better than inviting all your friends over and giving them a handful of freebies? HouseParty.com lets you do just that! They partner with companies like Febreeze, Hasbro, Canon, and more to bring you exclusive freebies, just for throwing a promotional party in your home. Visit their site for more information.

Free P&G Products To get free samples of everything from body wash to laundry detergent to toothpaste, go to PGEveryday.com and register to get free samples of Proctor & Gamble products. You'll also receive their excellent email newsletter, which has household tips and tricks as well as a wide variety of coupons.

Savings, Right at Home RightAtHome.com is a savings site by Johnson & Johnson. In addition to promoting their household products, they also have lots of great tips for organizing, crafts, cooking, and cleaning. The best part, of course, is their "Special offers" section, which has big coupons and free samples for products like Ziploc bags, Scrubbing Bubbles cleaner, Glade air fresheners, Windex window washing kits, Drano drain declogger, and more.

Free Gift Cards and More Recyclebank.com is our new favorite site to "mess around" on while watching TV. Dedicated to helping the environment, the site rewards you with points for liking Earth-friendly companies on Facebook, playing games, watching videos, and doing other green activities like pledging to recycle more. In return, you can exchange points for high-value coupons for organic products, free magazine subscriptions, and gift cards to such places as Panera Bread, Walmart, Old Navy, iTunes, and more.

Who Knew? Reader's Tip

If you have a kid who loves to collect stickers, you know that they'll save practically anything with a self-adhesive backing. For an extensive list of free stickers available online, Freaky Freddie is your go-to guy! Just visit FreakyFreddies.com/sticker .htm. They also list bumper stickers, in case it's time to plaster over that one from last year's election. —*Tammy Golding, via Facebook*

Prescriptions for Free If you don't have a prescription plan, or if your prescription plan has denied you coverage for an expensive medication, you may be able to get it for free or at a deep discount. NeedyMeds.com will tell you how to get the medicine you need from the government, private outreach programs, and even the pharmaceutical companies themselves. Just find the name of your medication in the "Brand name" or "Generics" list and see if you qualify! You should never be without the prescriptions you need.

. . . .

Swagbucks "It's like a frequent flyer mile for using the web," Swagbucks.com says about their internet rewards program. Swagbucks can be redeemed in their online store for video games, free MP3 downloads, toys, posters, office supplies, gift cards from major retailers, magazine subscriptions, and more. To earn Swagbucks, simply search the web from Search.Swagbucks.com and click on your point rewards when they pop up! You can also earn points by subscribing to their newsletter, following them on Facebook and Twitter, and taking surveys and polls. If you're interested in earning freebies easily online, this is the program for you.

. . . .

Free Patterns for Crafters Do you sew? Get free patterns from the leader in sewing—Butterick/McCall. Just go to Butterick.McCall.com/free-downloads-pages-1013.php. Sign up for their email program and get access to a wide variety of free patterns, most of which are for crafts. FreePatterns. com is also a great resource for patterns: They have free patterns for sewing, quilting, knitting, crocheting, and even paper crafts. If you're into knitting or crocheting, check out KnittingPatternCentral.com/directory.php for free knitting patterns of all sorts, including afghans, rugs, garments, toys, and just about anything you can think of. The Lion brand yarn company also offers free patterns if you join their site—just visit LionBrand.com/patterns. Other great sites for free knitting and crocheting patterns are FreeVintageKnitting.com and KnittingOnTheNet.com. A great crochet-only site is CrochetPatternCentral.com. And finally, if cross-stitching is your thing, get access to hundreds of free cross-stitching projects at Dawn's Cross Stitch. Just go to FreeCrossStitchPatternCentral.com and click on "Free pattern directory."

Household Products for Free If you love giving your opinion, you'll love Influenster.com. Try out new products for free in return for telling them what you think! The cool thing about the site is that the more reviews you post and share online, the more free products you'll qualify for!

Free Everything, from People Like You You can find hundreds of items—from furniture to books to clothes to exercise equipment—at Freecycle.org, a nonprofit website whose goal is to decrease landfill waste. Users join up and post about items they are giving away or need, and connect with other users who want the items or have what they're looking for. Just be careful—some free things are hard to resist, but do you really need that bedazzled couch cover?

Who Knew? Reader's Tip

Want to win a new computer, exotic getaway, gift cards, and more? Check out the Facebook page of Big Prize Giveaways (Facebook.com/bigprize) and enter to win one of their many contests. Big Prize Giveaways works with companies to spread the word about their products on Facebook. It's easy to enter, and you don't get hit with a ton of spam later. —*Maria Mendez, via Facebook*

Happy Birthday! If you're not sure what to do for your birthday, how about getting something for free? If we didn't offer you enough birthday deals in this book, head over to Free Birthday Treats, an easy, one-stop re-source of all things free on your birthday. Check it out at FreeBirthdayTreatsBlog.com.

chapter 9

Grocery Store Savings

· ·

Outsmart Sneaky Supermarkets

Look Down! When shelving items, grocery stores customarily put the least expensive items on the bottom shelves. That's because most customers, when looking for a particular product, will just take the first item they see—at eye level. When at the market, make sure to check the lower shelves for lower prices.

Supermarket Secret It's important to know that not *all* products are cheaper when you buy bigger sizes. Make sure to compare unit prices carefully at the store, because we have found that some items—like cereal and prepared frozen foods like french fries—are less expensive in smaller sizes. This is probably because the store knows these items are more likely to be purchased in bulk.

The Truth About Eggs White and brown eggs are identical in nutritional value and taste. Believe it or not, the only difference is that white eggs come from white chickens, and brown eggs come from brown chickens! When at the store, simply buy whatever is cheaper.

When a Deal Isn't a Deal When looking at your store's circular, be aware that not all of the products they show are on sale (even if they say "Deal!"). Stores often advertise a product just to call attention to it (like if they have too many in stock), not because it's on sale. So before you snatch up what you think is a deal, make sure to consider the prices of similar items.

Milk Matters Never buy milk in clear containers. When exposed to light, low-fat or skim milk can lose up to 70 percent of its vitamin A. Tinted or opaque containers will protect the vitamin A.

Sweet Savings To save money, purchase solid chocolate candy (usually in bunny or Santa form) after major holidays when it's gone on sale. Store the chocolate in the freezer, then shave off bits with a vegetable peeler to use on top of desserts.

Cheesy Secrets When buying cheese at the supermarket, make sure to check both the cheese section (usually by the deli counter) and the dairy section for the best prices. The dairy section will have much less expensive processed cheeses, while you may find a deal on an equivalent cheese in the cheese section. Also check at the deli counter to see if they're having any sales on cheddar, Munster, and other sandwich cheeses. You can always ask them to just cut you a slab if you are planning on cubing or shredding the cheese.

Can It Save at the store by going canned—all recipes except for salads and other raw dishes can be made with canned vegetables instead of the fresh ones. As long as you check the ingredients to make sure sugar hasn't been added, any vegetable in a can will taste nearly indistinguishable from a fresh one you cooked yourself, especially if it's going into sauces or casseroles.

Who Knew? Reader's Tip

Make sure to keep an eye on the prices at the salad bar. If you only need a few artichoke hearts or mozzarella balls for your recipe, they may be cheaper to buy there by the pound than elsewhere in the store. —*Colleen Levy Zaffiri, via Facebook*

Break Free from Brands When you've been buying the same brand-name product for as long as you can remember, it's hard to make the switch to generics. However, you'll be surprised when you find many generic and store-brand products taste exactly the same (or better!) for less than half the cost. Always buy generic baking ingredients such as flour, oil, and sugar. These generics are indistinguishable from their more-expensive counterparts. Frozen and canned vegetables are also usually exactly the same. As for products such as cereals, cookies, and crackers, basic is better—we've had good luck with plain granola, potato chips, and wheat crackers. No matter what the product, it never hurts to try. If you end up having to throw away one can of soup, you've wasted a few dollars, but if you like it, you can save a lot over the course of a year.

For Sundae Night Never, ever let us catch you buying sundae toppings in the ice-cream aisle! These nuts and mini candies are up to 50 percent cheaper in the baking aisle, which often has sprinkles, too. Melt some chocolate chips in a double boiler, then let them cool a bit and add to the top of ice cream for your own "instant shell."

Ham-Purchasing Secrets If you're going to buy a canned ham, purchase the largest one you can afford. Most smaller canned hams are made from bits and pieces glued together with gelatin. Cured hams are injected with a solution of brine salts, sugar, and nitrites. The weight of the ham will increase with the injection, and if the total weight goes up by 8 percent, the label will usually say "ham with natural juices." If the weight of the ham increases by more than 10 percent, the label must read "water added."

Market Watch Supermarkets have started using their own wording on meat packages to make you think that the product you are buying is a better grade than it really is. Most of the major chains are buying more select-grade beef, but may call it by any number of fancy names such as "top premium beef," "prime quality cut," "select choice," "market choice," or "premium cut." Be aware that these titles don't actually mean anything!

The Seasonal Secret The best way to save on produce is to buy fruits and veggies when they are in season. Any crop will be much cheaper when a farm near you is harvesting it, because the price won't include the transportation from another country. When a harvest has been particularly good, expect deep discounts as distributors try to get rid of a product before it goes bad. Visit EatTheSeasons.com to find out what produce is in season in the US and Canada.

Weighing In If you're buying produce that is priced by the item rather than by the pound (such as a head of lettuce, lemons, or avocados), take advantage of the store's

SAVINGS SECRETS
FOR MEAT

....

Leaner Isn't Always Better You don't always need to buy the leanest (and most expensive) ground beef. If you're preparing hamburgers on a grill or on a broiler rack, most of the fat will be lost during the cooking process, so stick with the moderately lean varieties.

....

Freezer Patties Never buy meat that's already been shaped into patties (unless it's on sale). Instead, buy your own and shape into patties yourself. Place a sheet of waxed paper between each, then place the entire stack in a resealable plastic bag and put it in the freezer.

....

Buy in Bulk You don't necessarily have to know how to butcher meat to buy in bulk—you can often ask the butcher to do it for you. Instead of pork tenderloin, try asking for an entire loin roast and ask the butcher to cut it into pieces.

....

Meat in the Mornings Looking for deals on meat? Hit up the supermarket in the early morning. That's when they'll be restocking the meat case, and you'll have the best chance of finding a deal.

....

Befriend the Butcher When does your supermarket mark down meat? It's as easy as asking the butcher. Especially if you're friendly, he or she will usually be happy to let you know this valuable savings secret.

scales and weigh them to find the heaviest one. This way, you'll be sure you're getting the most for your money.

Who Knew? Reader's Tip

When selecting limes or lemons at the market, go for the biggest you can find. They tend to be sweeter than their smaller counterparts.
—*Kate Higgins, via Twitter*

Corny Advice When corn is piled high in supermarket bins, go for the ears that are on top. Why? Corn gets rapidly less sweet the warmer it gets, and even the heat generated by all the corn on the top of the pile can make the corn on the bottom start to lose its deliciously sweet taste.

Avoid Frosted Vegetables When shopping in the freezer aisle, avoid packages of frozen vegetables that have frost on them. It's a sign that the food has thawed and refrozen, and a percentage of moisture has already been lost. You should also give bags of frozen food a quick squeeze before putting them in your cart. If the food is solid, it has thawed and refrozen and should be avoided.

When and Where to Shop

Go for the Big Haul Buying lots of groceries in one trip rather than a few groceries in several trips is better for your wallet. Not only do you save on gas money, but according to a study by the Marketing Science Institute, shoppers who are only making a quick trip to the store purchase an average of 54 percent more than they had planned. In addition to visiting the store less frequently, make a grocery list before you go cut down on impulse buys.

Save with Seconds Supermarkets often discount their day-old or slightly overripe items in the morning. This is a great way of getting deals on fruit, vegetables, bread, and other foods. At first glimpse, this money-saving strategy may not seem appealing to you, but you can use these items in casseroles, desserts, and other dishes where you won't even notice the difference. With a loaf of day-old bread, for example, you can make french toast, stuffing, croutons, bread pudding, and much more!

Why Not Try Wednesday? For a relaxing shopping experience, hit the supermarket on a Wednesday. Fewer people do their grocery shopping on this day than any other day, so the aisles will be less crowded, leaving you more room to roam. Who knew?

Never Pay a Dollar for a Lemon Again It may be a pain, but the best way to save on groceries is to shop at more than one market. You'll soon find that one store will have cheaper produce, one will have cheaper meat, and so forth. Explore grocery stores you've never shopped at—perhaps one that is closer to your workplace or gym rather than by your home—and you may find even lower prices. We've even found cheaper products at stores that are the same chain, just a different location. Write down the prices of your most frequently purchased items, or bring a receipt from an average grocery trip with you. That way you can be sure to remember where the prices are the most reasonable.

New Stores Spell New Savings Anytime a new grocery store opens up in our area, we always stop by to take a look. It may be a pain to navigate differently laid-out aisles, but new supermarkets offer big sales and the lowest prices possible in their first few weeks and months of business as an incentive to get shoppers to switch stores. Many stores also offer contests and giveaways to celebrate their grand openings, so visiting during the first week is a good idea.

Beyond Grocery Stores When hunting for the best prices, don't let your journey stop at the supermarket. Sometimes, stores that don't specialize in groceries will actually give you the lowest price on some staples. For instance, a nearby gas station or convenience store might have a special price on milk or soda to get customers inside. CVS, Walgreens, and other drugstores are also good places to buy certain foods, such as soup, spaghetti sauce, and candy. Make sure to take a walk down these stores' food aisles and compare the prices to your regular supermarket, especially the food that's on sale. Another great place to find low prices on food is at your local dollar store.

Go Native Especially in cities, stores by and for immigrants abound. Whether it's a Mexican, Indian, Ethiopian, Chinese, or Korean grocery, you'll find cheap deals on foods that are native to that country. Bulk spices can be especially cheap, and you'll also find items such as inexpensive tortillas and avocados. We never buy rice unless it's from an ethnic market, as it's usually up to 80 percent cheaper than buying it at the grocery store.

....

Not Just Members Only Just because you don't belong to a wholesale club doesn't necessarily mean you can't shop there. Many states have laws that say that a store must allow anyone (even non-members) to buy prescription medication and/or alcohol there. Most stores will also allow you to shop there if a friend has given you a gift card for the store. Call the store's customer service department and ask them what their policy is.

Maximizing Your Coupon Savings

• •

Clip-Free Coupons Clipping coupons doesn't have to include scissors! Check out your supermarket's website to see if they allow you to virtually clip coupons by selecting them on the site and then "adding" them to your store loyalty card. When they scan your card at the store, you'll automatically get the savings! If you shop at a big chain, there's a good chance you can add coupons to your card at other sites, too. Some good sites to check out are Coupons.com, RedPlum.com, and Cellfire.com. Many of them even have mobile apps.

Take a Coupon, Leave a Coupon Can't get enough coupons? How about making a "Take a Coupon, Leave a Coupon" box? Set it up at your office, or ask your library or a local cafe if you can place one there. Everyone leaves coupons they can't use, and takes what they can.

Get Chatty About Coupons Believe it or not, one of the best places to get coupons is still your Sunday paper. But what if you've started clipping coupons, and even printed them out from the internet, but you still don't feel like you have enough to make a dent in your grocery bill? Make sure your coworkers, friends, relatives, and neighbors all know that you're a coupon-clipper, and ask them to save any coupon inserts they have. Perhaps it's their guilt at not taking advantage of coupons themselves, but you'll be surprised how many extra coupons you'll receive from others who don't mind lending a hand to help you save.

One Per Purchase If you've ever seen the common limitation "limit one per purchase" on a coupon, you may have thought that you could only use one of these coupons during a shopping trip. But that isn't true! The limitation actually means that you can only use one of these coupons per item, not per trip. For example, if you're buying five tubes of toothpaste and you have five identical coupons, you can use all of them. This is important to keep in mind if you find a great deal on an item you buy regularly. Get a second newspaper or have a friend save hers, and you can now get double the discount! Then stockpile your items and save.

Trial-Size Treasures If you're used to checking the "unit" prices of items at the grocery store, you know that buying the bigger size almost always means a better value. But when you have coupons, the opposite is usually true. That's because with couponing, the name of the game is getting the biggest percentage off your purchase. For instance, if you have a $1 coupon and buy the product that

costs $2, you're getting half off. But if you buy the prod-
uct that costs $2.50, you're only getting 40 percent off.
This method can pay off big in your store's trial-size aisle.
If your coupon says "any size" (and doesn't exclude trial
sizes), you'll often find that you can get 60–95 percent off
your purchase when you buy a trial size. Buy several trial
sizes with several coupons and you have the same amount
of product as you would with a regular size—at a fraction
of the cost.

Coupon Matchups Taking your couponing from casual
to extreme is all about one thing: matchups! "Matchup" is
couponer slang for when a coupon you have matches up
with an in-store sale or other coupons. These sales usually
happen three to four weeks after a coupon has been released. Luckily, there's an easy way to find out if coupons
you have are matching up with any sales: Simply Google
the name of the supermarket where you shop and the
words "coupon matchups." There are a plethora of helpful
coupon bloggers out there who will tell you what's on sale
and what recent coupons are for the same products!

Double Trouble You can save big (twice as much, in
fact) if you shop at a grocery store that doubles coupons—
that is, offers you $1 off for using a 50¢-off coupon.
Unfortunately, these stores are few and far between in

most states. Visit Couponing.about.com/od/groceryzone/a/doublecoupons.htm for a reader-generated list of stores that double. And if you find one, consider yourself lucky!

Who Knew? Reader's Tip

My favorite place to get coupons is *All You* magazine. It contains anywhere from $40–$100 worth of coupons each month! Look for subscription deals online—you can usually get it for less than $2 per issue. —*Dawn Mason, via Facebook*

Print Smart If you print out coupons from sites like Coupons.com, here's a secret you'll want to know: You can print out most internet coupons two times from each computer. Just click your internet browser's "Back" button, or go back to the site's homepage and search for the coupon again. If you have another computer in your home, you can print two more coupons from that computer!

Clever Couponing Don't mind clipping coupons, but don't have the time to leaf through inserts full of products you don't use? Sign up at Rather-Be-Shopping.com to receive email alerts when coupons for brands you buy are released, both in your local paper and on the internet.

COMPANIES THAT GIVE AWAY COUPONS

We Love Betty Crocker Get coupons for Betty Crocker products—as well as Bisquick, Green Giant, Hamburger Helper, and more—straight from Betty's Crocker's website at BettyCrocker.com/coupons-promotions

All-in-One-Source Live Better America is an initiative by a family of brands including Cheerios, Yoplait, Progresso, Fruit Roll-Ups, Nature Valley, Johnson & Johnson, Ziploc, and Windex. Find coupons for all of these products and more at LiveBetterAmerica.com/coupons.

Get Your Vitamins Vitamins are important to our health, which is why we're happy NatureMade is so generous with their online coupons. Get them at NatureMade.com/Promotions-and-Special-Offers/Coupon-Center.

Cereal and More Get coupons for Kellogg's cereals, as well as their yummy Keebler and Morningstar Farms products at Kelloggs.com/en_US/coupon.html

A Trusted Brand Arm & Hammer not only offers coupons for baking soda, but on toothpaste, deodorant, cat litter, and more. Find them at ArmAndHammer.com/resources/savings center.aspx.

Free Food Secrets

● ●

Free Food from Kraft At KraftFirstTaste.com, you can sign up to sample new products from Kraft Foods. After registering with the site, click on the "My offers" section to see what freebies are available. You'll have to answer a survey to get your freebies, and like most freebie sites with surveys, you'll have to answer "correctly" if you want your free sample. For example, if you say you never buy cream cheese, you probably won't be eligible to receive a free sample of Philadelphia cream cheese!

New Product Freebies Want to get free General Mills food products, which includes brands like Pillsbury, Betty Crocker, and Bisquick? Join their product testing panel at MillsAdvisoryPanel.com. They'll send you free samples and coupons of new products in exchange for filling out an online survey about your experience. McCormick also has some opportunities for home-testers of their spices; go to McCormickCorporation.com/contactus/consumertesting. aspx for more information.

Five Years of Spice Who wouldn't love this deal? If you buy specially marked spice racks from Kamenstein, Farberware, KitchenAid, or Cuisinart, you can get free replacement spices for five years! Choose from more than 30 herbs and spices, and pay only a small shipping cost. To learn more about the program, visit Pfaltzgraff.com/Free-Spices/free_spices,default,sc.html.

· ·

Free Coffee! They say there's no such thing as a free lunch, but we've found a few places to get a free cup of joe! If you have a Starbucks card, which is a refillable cash card, you can get a free refill on brewed coffee or tea. Plus, if you register your card, you can get rewards points toward free food and drinks. Additionally, most Dunkin' Donuts locations also have a rewards program that allows you to earn free coffee. Both IHOP and Panera also offer free coffee refills during a single visit. To find more places near you that offer free refills of all kinds of beverages, check out Yelp.com, and search for "free refill" or "bottomless."

· ·

Great for Date Nights OpenTable.com is not only convenient for making reservations at thousands of restaurants nationwide, they also give you freebies! Earn points each time you make a reservation, then redeem them for a free meal at any of their partner restaurants. Another great site for getting money back on meals is RewardsNetwork.com. They give you points and money back on your tab at restaurants nationwide.

· ·

Free Restaurant Freebies Lots of restaurants—from sit-down places to fast food joints—offer free food for signing up for their email list. Check the website of your favorite restaurant or ask the next time you're visiting. Some restaurants that offer free food as part of a loyalty program are the Olive Garden, TGI Friday's, Houlihan's, Moe's Southwest Grill, Qdoba, Orange Julius, Dairy Queen, Friendly's, Schlotzsky's, and IHOP.

Who Knew? Reader's Tip

If you're a chocoholic, your next stop online should be Godiva.com/rewards, where you can register for Godiva Chocolatier's member rewards program. Just for signing up, you'll receive a free chocolate every time you walk into a Godiva store! (Limit one per month.) You'll also get free gifts when you buy chocolate online and in-store. Make sure to log in on the 16th of each month, when you get an additional freebie when you order on-line. —*Jo Ann Caracci, via WhoKnewTips.com*

The 411 on Food Freebies Want to know where the Burger King free sample truck is going to stop, which fast food joints are giving away free food on Tax Day, how to get free coupons to Olive Garden, and when new deals are being released at chain restaurants? Look no further than

EatDrinkDeals.com. They're a great all-in-one source for restaurant coupons, sales, and other promotions. You'll never have to eat out at full price again!

Free Meals for Kids Many restaurants offer free meals for kids on particular days each week. To find a bunch in your area, visit KidsMealDeals.com. Enter your zip code and you'll find deals from chain restaurants and local joints alike, and they even have apps for iPhones and Blackberrys in case you need it on-the-go.

DIY Money-Savers in the Kitchen

Tea Saver Want to get more for your money when it comes to tea? Always buy the loose variety, and then use one-third of what's recommended. Just let the tea steep a little longer, and it will taste exactly the same as if you used the full amount.

DIY Instant Waffles For a quick and healthy breakfast, make waffles ahead of time, then freeze them. When you or your family is ready to eat, pop them in the toaster to reheat. Making waffles from scratch, rather than buying them in the frozen foods section, will save you money. You can also easily do this with French toast!

Don't Pay for "Instant" If you're hooked on instant oatmeal packets, try this trick instead for big savings. Buy instant oats in bulk, then in a sandwich bag combine ¼ cup oats with ½ teaspoon each of sugar and cinnamon, and a pinch of salt. Pre-pack several and you're set for the week!

Easy, Sweet Coffee If you love sweetened, flavored coffee, simply mix ¼ teaspoon vanilla extract or 1 teaspoon cinnamon with 1 cup sugar in a food processor until well blended, then add a little scoop to your next cup. It's usually much cheaper than buying flavored coffees or creamers, and tastes better, too.

Craft Your Own Coffee Filters Does your coffeemaker require cone-shaped filters? Save some cash by purchasing the less expensive round filters in bulk. You can buy a 500-pack for cheap, then shape the filters into cones so they fit your machine. With a few simple folds, they work just as well as the pricier alternatives.

Syrup Substitute Out of maple syrup and still want to make waffles this morning? Try this delicious substitute. Combine ⅓ cup butter, ⅓ cup sugar, and half a can of frozen orange juice concentrate in a saucepan. Cook over medium heat, stirring constantly, until the sugar has dissolved and the mixture is syrupy.

Who Knew? Reader's Tip

It's a pain to dig out the last dregs from a peanut butter jar, but a waste to throw them out. So don't do either one. Instead use the jar as a take-along breakfast container by adding instant oatmeal, dried fruits, and nuts. When it's time to eat all you have to do is add hot water, close, and shake. So easy and nothing extra to clean up!

—*Melissa Massaro, via Facebook*

We Can't Believe It's Not Butter The problem: You love store-bought butter spreads, but you know the trans fats inside aren't good for you. The solution? Make your own at home! Just combine a stick of butter and ¼ cup canola oil with a hand mixer. It will be soft and easy to spread! If you buy them in bulk, you can also save money over buying store-bought margarine.

Double Your Frosting You may not have time to make your own frosting, but you can blend store-bought frosting with a hand mixer to double the volume. This simple little trick saves money and calories!

Who Knew? Reader's Tip

Making a treat that calls for a pretty layer of sprinkled confectioner's sugar? Create a sugar shaker by poking tiny holes in the bottom of a plastic cup. Pour sugar into the homemade shaker, and sprinkle it over the dessert.

—Sherrie Pawlowski, via Facebook

Easily Make Your Own Bread Crumbs Don't spend money on store-bought bread crumbs. Set aside a special jar and pour in the crumbs from the bottom of cracker or low-sugar cereal boxes. Also add crumbs from leftover garlic bread and a few dried herbs, and soon you'll have seasoned bread crumbs! The great thing is that homemade bread crumbs are even better than store-bought, since their uneven texture helps make them stick.

Super Sharpening Tip If you don't own a knife sharpener, you can still keep your kitchen knives at their best without taking them to a professional. All you need is a mug or plate with an unglazed rim on the bottom! Holding your knife at a 20-degree angle, slide your knife blade along the edge of the rim from handle to tip. Continue making passes along this rim until the knife is the desired sharpness, and then repeat on the other side. A sharp knife should easily slice through a tomato or piece of paper without snagging.

Who Knew? Reader's Tip

Microwave popcorn is convenient, but it also contains lots of chemicals and preservatives. Make a healthier, cheaper version yourself! Place ⅓ cup plain kernels in a brown paper bag, and fold over several times to close tightly (you might even want to staple it shut). Then stick the bag in the microwave on the popcorn setting. (It may take more or less time for the kernels to pop, so watch it closely.) Remove, and season as desired.

—*Mike Comella, via Facebook*

Best Croutons Ever If you really want to impress your dinner guests, make some homemade croutons for your salad. After cutting your leftover bread into cubes, fry in olive oil and a little garlic powder (not garlic salt), a pinch of Parmesan cheese, and parsley. Fry until they're brown, then let cool on paper towels. You can also cut the bread into smaller pieces, then chop in a blender or food processor to make bread crumbs (you may have to cut off the bottom crust first).

···

From Whole to Chopped Your supermarket has only canned whole tomatoes, and you need chopped! Don't take out each tomato and make a mess on your cutting board. Instead, simply insert a clean pair of scissors into the can and snip.

Who Knew? Reader's Tip

When preparing a recipe that requires you to drain something you've just cooked on several layers of paper towels to absorb the grease, use this trick to waste fewer paper towels. Lay down several sheets of old newspaper, then place a single layer of paper towels on top.

—*Shannon Reynik, via WhoKnewTips.com*

Stock Up on Stock When carving a chicken or turkey, it's easy to make a stock at the same time. Place all unused parts in a pot with celery and onion (using the skins of the onion will give the stock a nice, rich color), then heat up to boiling. Reduce the heat and simmer while you make dinner. Then turn off and skim the fat when cooled. Stock can be used for gravies, made into soup (naturally), and used to flavor rice, potatoes, and tomato sauce. This free and easy seasoning would have cost you up to $5 for a quart at the grocery store!

Stock-Freezing Secrets If you're making a large batch of soup or stock and need to store the leftovers, pour the remaining soup into plastic bags. Here's the easy way to do it: Line a drinking glass with a resealable plastic bag. Pour the stock into the glass until it's about three-quarters full, then seal the bag and lay flat on a baking pan on the bottom of your freezer. Once they're frozen, stack them on top of one another for optimal storage that'll save you valuable freezer space. Defrost by peeling off the bag and placing in a covered casserole dish in the microwave. A sandwich-sized bag holds approximately a cup, so defrost only what you need and the rest will last longer!

Pringles Can for Pasta Glass jars specifically designed to store pasta can be pretty, but they can also be pretty expensive. If you're looking for an easy and cheap way to store pasta, try an old Pringles container! It's the perfect size for spaghetti, linguini, and other long pasta. If you want, pretty it up by adding some wrapping or contact paper to the outside.

Keep a Food Thermometer in Place Using a food thermometer to cook a dish in a large pot? You won't have to juggle your stirring spoon and your thermometer using this handy-dandy binder clip tip! Make your thermometer stand upright on its own by sliding one metal prong on your clip over the base of the thermometer; then secure the clip to the edge of the pot. Your hands are free to stir, and you don't need to stand over the pot waiting for your temp to climb.

Tenderizing Trick To tenderize tough meat without store-bought tenderizer, use baking soda. Just rub baking soda all over the meat, refrigerate for a few hours, and rinse well before cooking.

Making Food Last Longer

Herbal Life For a delicious way to preserve the bounty of summer herbs, try making a compound butter. First, allow a stick of butter to soften on the counter. Meanwhile, chop up some of your favorite herbs. Then blend together the herbs and the softened butter with a food processor or hand mixer. Turn the mixture out onto parchment paper, and roll it into a log. Place the log in a freezer bag, and freeze for up to several months. Whenever you want a taste of summer, just cut off a small piece and use on steaks, bread, and sautéed vegetables. Delicious!

Bacon Wrapper If you're cooking less than a full package of bacon, how do you store the extra slices? Just roll each slice into a tight cylinder, place in an airtight plastic bag, and freeze. Simply thaw and unroll when you're ready to cook!

Who Knew? Reader's Tip

When freezing burgers or chops, put sheets of parchment paper between each item before storing in freezer bags. The paper makes it easy to remove the meat when it's time to cook. As an alternative to parchment paper, repurpose coffee can lids.
—*Caren C., via email*

Keep Onions Fresh The sugar content of yellow onions makes them spoil quickly if they are stored closely together—who knew? The solution is to store your onions in an old (clean) pair of pantyhose, making knots in the legs so the onions can't touch. It might look a little weird, but it works!

Making Tomatoes Last For the best storage, keep tomatoes stem-side down in a cool place (but not the fridge, which is so cold it will rupture the tomato's delicate cells). Try to keep them from touching, but if they are still attached to the stem, it's best to leave them that way.

Leftover Rice, Longer Rice can be stored in fridge for a longer amount of time if you store a slice of toast on top of it. The toast will absorb excess moisture and keep the rice fluffy and fresh.

Freezing Bread If you find that your bread often goes stale before you use it, slice it and store in the freezer. Separate out slices and let them sit for about five minutes at room temperature to defrost, or stick them directly in the toaster. Frozen bread is also great to use for grilled cheese sandwiches—it's much easier to butter, and it will defrost as it cooks in the pan.

Don't Let Apples Go to Waste If you have a bunch of apples that are going to go bad soon, here's how you can use them up quickly: Cut them into wedges or smaller chunks, dump them in a saucepan, and sauté them in butter over medium heat. When that's finished, sprinkle a half sugar/half cinnamon mixture on top, and you've got a yummy treat that the kids will love. You can even use them as the start of a homemade apple pie!

Bread Loves Celery Strange but true: Bread stays fresh for a longer time if you place it in an airtight bag with a stalk of celery.

Who Knew? Reader's Tip

Keep sliced apples from browning in your kid's lunch box with a rubber band! Hold the apple together while slicing (using an apple slicer works best), then secure the rubber band around it to hold it together. The cut edges will stay on the inside until your child takes off the rubber band!
—*Lynne Kolimago, via WhoKnewTips.com*

Keep Potatoes Fresh If you store fresh ginger with potatoes it will help keep them fresh longer. Half an apple stored with potatoes will stop them from sprouting by absorbing moisture before the potato does.

Water Your Asparagus! To make asparagus last longer in the refrigerator, place the stem ends in a container of water, or wrap them in a wet paper towel and put in a plastic bag. Like flowers, the asparagus will continue "drinking" the water and stay fresh until they're ready to use.

Lasting Lemons You bought a bunch of lemons on sale, but now they've only got a day or two before they go bad. Put them to good use—later—by slicing them up and placing them in muffin tins. Cover each muffin tin cup with water, then freeze and pop out into a Ziploc bag. Then drop into ice water for a refreshing treat!

Save Some Zest for Later Don't discard the rinds of limes, lemons, oranges, or other citrus fruits. Grate them, then store in tightly covered glass jars in the fridge. They make excellent flavorings for cakes and can be sprinkled over chicken and fish as well.

Foil Foible Never wrap foods that contain natural acids—like tomatoes, lemons, or onions—in aluminum foil. The combination of the foil and the acid in the foods produces a chemical reaction, which affects the taste of the food.

Mold-Free Melons To keep melons from getting moldy as they ripen, rub the exterior peel with a teaspoon of white vinegar every few days.

Raisin Rejuvenation Sad-looking raisins? To plump them up to perfection, place them a small baking dish with a little water, cover, and bake in a preheated 325°F oven for 6–8 minutes. Or, pour boiling water over the raisins and let them stand for 10–15 minutes.

Revive Limp Celery Have you ever found it hard to use up an entire package of celery before it starts going all rubbery on you? To get the celery crispy again, place it in a bowl of ice water with a few slices of potato, then wait an hour. When you come back to it, it will be ready to use.

Who Knew? Reader's Tip

You can keep celery lasting even longer in your refrigerator by taking it out of its original packaging and wrapping it in aluminum foil!

—*Jimmy Jenkins, via letter*

Banish Bugs from Cauliflower Eliminate the bugs that sometimes make their home in cauliflower by soaking the head upside down in salt water for half an hour. Then simply lift the head up straight up out of the water. The little bugs will stay behind in the bowl, and you can use the cauliflower as usual.

Fresh Vs. Dried We've all been in this situation: You want to make a particular recipe, but you only have the dried form of the herb called for. Save yourself a trip to the supermarket with this handy rule of thumb. When using dried, use a third of the amount that's called for of the fresh herb, and vice versa. For example, 1 tablespoon fresh oregano equals 1 teaspoon dried.

Who Knew? Reader's Tip

Your lettuce will last longer if you store it in a bag with a piece of nearly burnt toast. Yes, really! The toast will absorb moisture from the lettuce, making it last a long time. Check the toast daily, and replace it once it gets soggy.

—*Jessica Krause-Cowling, via Facebook*

Making Condiments Last It's frustrating to have to throw out condiments like sour cream, mayo, yogurt, and mustard because you didn't use the entire container before it went bad. However, you can easily combat this by changing containers as you use up the item. Using a smaller container exposes the condiment to less air—and fewer bacteria. The trick, of course, is making sure you successfully transfer every bit of mayo possible from the jar to the tiny Tupperware. We usually do our container downsizing right before we're about to use the condiment on something. That way, we can scrape out what we don't transfer for our sandwiches.

Who Knew? Reader's Tip

Store brown sugar in the freezer and lumps will be a thing of the past!
—*Chelsea Forshay, via WhoKnewTips.com*

Birth of a Logo Before you put away that carton of eggs, turn the container upside down. Storing eggs with the tapered end down maximizes the distance between the yolk and the air pocket, which may contain bacteria. The yolk is more perishable than the white, and turning the eggs upside down will change their center of gravity, and the yolk will move away from possible contamination. This means your eggs will last even longer!

Save Your Eggs Have a recipe that calls for egg whites only? Believe it or not, you can save egg yolks for later use. If you have used egg whites in a recipe and want to save the yolks, slide them into a bowl of water, cover with plastic wrap, and store in the refrigerator for a day or two. To keep them for longer, you can freeze separated eggs in a lightly oiled ice-cube tray. When frozen, pop them out and store in separate Ziploc bags in the freezer. These fro-

TIPS FOR
REFRIGERATOR FOODS

Storing Dairy Products It's better to store milk on an inside shelf toward the back of the refrigerator, not on the door. Why? All dairy products are very perishable. The optimal refrigeration temperature is actually just over 32°F; however, few refrigerators are ever set at or hold that low a temperature. Most home refrigerators remain around 40°F, and the temperature rises every time the door is opened.

Separate Drawers If possible, store fruits and vegetables in separate drawers in your fridge. Even when chilled, fruits give off ethylene gas that shortens the shelf life of vegetables (and other fruit) by causing them to ripen more quickly.

Where's the Cheese? Store cheese near the bottom of the refrigerator, where temperature fluctuations are minimal.

Better Butter Flavor Inside the fridge, margarine and butter quickly absorb odors from other foods. Make sure you always keep them tightly sealed to keep them at their best quality.

Egg-Cellent Answers To avoid the absorption of refrigerator odors, always store eggs in their original carton on an inside shelf of the refrigerator.

zen eggs are better for baking than for breakfast, but it's a great solution for eggs that are about to go bad.

Keep Cheese Fresher! To keep cheese fresh and moist, wrap it in a cloth dampened in white vinegar and put it in an airtight container.

Who Knew? Reader's Tip

Before you store semi-hard cheeses like Cheddar, Swiss, or Gruyère, rub the cut edges with a little bit of butter. You'll never notice the taste difference, and the cheese will be less likely to dry out or become moldy.   —*Karen Bauder, via email*

Cottage Cheese Care Because of its high water content, cottage cheese doesn't last as long as other food products in the refrigerator. To extend its life, store it in the container upside down.

Cheese Freeze Believe it or not, you can successfully freeze many varieties of cheese without them losing their taste or texture. Cut into small blocks, place in sealed plastic bags, and then keep in the freezer for when you need them. Cheese varieties that can be successfully frozen are brick, cheddar, Camembert, Edam, Gouda, Muenster, Parmesan, Port du Salut, Swiss, provolone, mozzarella, and Romano. Small cheeses, such as Camembert, can even be frozen in their original packages. When removed from the freezer, cheese should be put in the refrigerator and used as soon as possible after thawing.

A Cottage Cheese Shortcut When making meatballs, meatloaf, or hamburger patties, try adding ½ cup cottage cheese for every pound of ground meat. Not only does it add flavor and protein, but it will stretch your recipe to serve a few more people.

Preserving Sour Cream To help sour cream last longer, add white vinegar right after you open it (1 teaspoon for a small container and 2 tablespoons for a large container). You won't notice the taste, and the sour cream won't go bad as quickly.

Pop Every Kernel Are your popcorn kernels too pooped to pop? It's probably because they have lost too much moisture, but they can be revived. Soak the kernels in water for five minutes, then dry them off and try again. Or freeze them overnight and pop them when frozen.

Can the Pam Never pay for aerosol cooking sprays. Instead, buy a giant jug of vegetable oil and add it to a clean spray bottle as needed. It's the same thing and will cost a fraction of the price.

How to Conserve Cooking Oil The next time you buy a bottle of cooking oil, don't remove the entire safety seal. Instead, make a small slit in it with a knife and take off only a small sliver. It's like making your own pouring spout! You'll cut back on those greasy drips down the side of the bottle, and since you'll be pouring more slowly, you'll use less.

Who Knew? Reader's Tip

To make the bubbles in your soda last longer, decrease the amount of air that the carbon dioxide (which causes the fizz) has to escape into. This is easily accomplished by squeezing in the sides of the bottle after you pour a glass.

—*Tanya Santos, via Facebook*

Fizz Trick Yes, there *is* a way to keep open soda from going flat. Not for a month, but for an hour or so. Leave an open can or bottle inside a sealed plastic freezer bag while you run out to do your errands, and it will still be bubbly when you get back.

....

Keep Leftover Cake Moist If you have leftover cake, you have more self-control than we do! One of the best methods of keeping the insides of a cake from drying out is to place a piece of fresh white bread next to the exposed surface. The bread can be affixed with a toothpick or a short piece of spaghetti.

Who Knew? Reader's Tip

To keep your cookies tasting chewy until the last one is eaten, add half an apple or a slice of white bread to the cookie jar. This will provide just enough moisture to keep the cookies from becoming hard.   —*Teresa Moore, via email*

Keep Ice Off Your Ice Cream It's always disappointing when you remember you have one last bit of ice cream in the freezer, only to open it and find it's covered in ice crystals. To keep this from happening, simply store your ice cream container upside-down.

....

The Best Beans for Your Brew Unlike other kinds of coffee beans, fresh-roasted coffee beans should not be stored in airtight containers. Fresh-roasted beans are usually packed in bags that are not airtight, allowing the carbon monoxide formed during the roasting process to escape. If the carbon monoxide doesn't escape, the coffee will have a poor taste.

What You Never Knew About Milk When you know your milk is going to go bad before you can use up the rest of it, separate it out into a few resealable containers and put them in your freezer. That's right, milk can be frozen! If you use skim milk, it can be thawed and drunk later, and you'll never be able to tell the difference in taste. For other varieties of milk, after thawing, use for sauces or baking. This is a great strategy for when you find milk at a deep discount. Buy as much as you can and freeze for later!

Who Knew? Reader's Tip

Adding a teaspoon of baking soda or a pinch of salt to a carton of milk will keep it fresh for a week or so past its expiration date.
—*Jennifer Kerins, via Facebook*

chapter 10

Saving on Makeup and Cosmetics

· ·

DIY Makeup and Cosmetics

Homemade Hints for
Healthy Hair

Savings Secrets for
Beauty Products

DIY Makeup and Cosmetics

All-Natural Freshening Face Cleanser We love this easy homemade face wash, which doubles as an exfoliator that leaves your skin feeling softer and smoother than before. Mix 1 tablespoon baking soda with enough lemon juice to create a paste, then rub all over your face. Leave for a few minutes so the mild acids in the lemon and baking soda can get to work. Lemon is a natural disinfectant and, combined with the gentle exfoliating powers of the baking soda, it'll clean, tone, and even out your skin as well as unclog your pores—say good-bye to blackheads!

Avocado-Honey Mask This gooey concoction does wonders to rehydrate our flaky winter-worn skin. Mix ½ mashed ripe avocado with ¼ cup honey, then apply to face and leave for 10 minutes. Wipe clean with a washcloth dipped in face soap.

Almond-Milk Wrinkle Wrangler We're always looking for new skin treatments that we can make at home. One of our favorite ingredients? Almonds. Not only do they moisturize and infuse skin with vitamins and antioxidants, they also fight wrinkles and prevent other signs of aging. This almond mask is an excellent (and yummy) treatment for your face. Place 5 raw almonds in 1 cup milk; let sit overnight. Remove the soaked almonds and grind them, then gradually add the almond-infused milk until a paste is formed. Add 2 tablespoons honey; stir. Rub the paste onto your skin and leave for up to 20 minutes.

Who Knew? Reader's Tip

Don't buy one of those toothpaste clips you see at stores. You can use a binder clip instead! If your tube of toothpaste is unwieldy and you're finding it difficult to squeeze out remaining paste, this trick will help with easy dispensing: Make sure the tube is securely capped, then squeeze the toothpaste up to the top of the tube, roll up the flat, empty end, and clamp it closed with a binder clip.
—*Joe Gallagher, via Facebook*

Don't Pay for "Dark Spot Corrector" We'll admit it, this sounds like a dip for chips, but it's actually a great mask that's ideal for lightening dark spots on your face while still being very gentle on skin. Mix together ¼ cup sour cream and 2 teaspoons parsley in a small bowl, and apply to clean skin. Leave for about 15 minutes, and rinse with cool water. You can leave leftover mask in the fridge; repeat nightly for several weeks to see results.

Kiwi Fruit for Your Face Kiwis are a deliciously sweet summertime fruit, but did you know that they're also great for your skin? Loads of antioxidants, exfoliating enzymes, and vitamin C make kiwi an easy choice for an all-natural homemade face scrub. Here's how we make our very basic kiwi exfoliant: Peel and cut 1 thin slice from a kiwi fruit (you can eat the rest!). Mash the pulp and massage it over your face as you would with your regular cleanser. Leave it on for up to 15 minutes, then rinse.

Never Buy Face Powder Again Make your own loose face powder with cornstarch! After all, most commercial powders, whether drugstore brands or pricey makeup counter options, use cornstarch as a base. To add color, sprinkle in a little cocoa powder until you get your desired shade. Store it in a pretty tin, and use just as you would your usual loose powder. Not only have you saved money, you've made an all-natural face product that doesn't contain a single chemical.

Egg-White Wash for Smaller Pores Here's another great straight-from-the-kitchen skin-care solution—this time, we'll tackle large, dirt-clogged pores. While we can't physically reduce the size of our pores (thanks, genetics!), we *can* make them look smaller. Try this technique once or twice per week: Whip egg whites from one egg together

HOMEMADE TONERS

Watermelon for Oily Skin Full of pore-cleaning amino acids, watermelon juice is great for oily skin. Make a great summer toner with this miracle ingredient by mixing together 3 tablespoons watermelon juice (either use a juicer or press the flesh through a strainer) with 3 tablespoons water and 3 tablespoons witch hazel, a powerful astringent that can be found at most drugstores. Store extra in the fridge.

Pineapple Power In a small bottle, mix together 1 cup filtered water with 2 tablespoons pineapple juice and 1 crushed-up vitamin C tablet. Close, and shake until the tablet is dissolved. Apply to freshly cleansed skin for tighter pores and fewer breakouts. Keep the toner refrigerated—it feels even better against skin when it's cold!

Acne-Fighting Tea Treatment The white tea in this toner boasts anti-inflammatory and anti-aging powers. Simply combine ⅓ cup hot white tea and ⅓ cup apple cider vinegar.

Purifying Parsley Here's a great way to get rid of leftover parsley while making a cooling facial spray that will purify pores. Finely chop about ½ cup parsley and place in a small bowl. Pour 1 cup of boiling water over the parsley, and allow the mixture to steep for 10–15 minutes before straining. Store in the fridge.

with 1 teaspoon cornstarch. When the mixture is frothy, rub onto your face and leave for 20 minutes. When it's dry, wash off with warm water.

A Sticky Trick for Pores Don't buy expensive pore strips for blackheads. Raid your child's school supplies instead! Apply a thin film of white glue to your nose and other problem areas. Allow to dry, and peel off to reveal cleaner pores.

Gentle Lip Scrub Cut out the "middle man" of expensive lip balms that contain vitamin E and go straight to the source! Buy some vitamin E capsules at a health-food or vitamin store and use them directly on your lips. Just squeeze out the contents of the capsule and apply to lips, or make this simple lip scrub that's both exfoliating and moisturizing—ideal for sensitive skin. Mix the contents of a vitamin E capsule with enough sugar to make a paste. Rub onto your lips for 30 seconds, then wait three minutes before rinsing with warm water.

Plump Up the Volume Even those amazing plumping lipsticks can be made at home. For lips worthy of Angelina Jolie, try this plumping balm. Melt the 3 tablespoons beeswax and 1 tablespoon vegetable oil in a double boiler. Using a rasp grater, grate a teaspoon of ginger onto a piece of cheesecloth. Squeeze the cheesecloth over the wax mixture to release some of the fragrant ginger juices, and stir to combine. Keep the balm in a small container (save used-up lip balm containers, or use a travel case for contacts), and spread a little on your lips anytime you want a little extra boost! The ginger will not only plump your lips, it will smell wonderful. Don't forget to make extra for jealous friends!

Who Knew? Reader's Tip

You can make your own lip gloss with Crystal Light powdered drink mix. In a bowl, add a small amount of petroleum jelly and a few sprinkles of your favorite flavor of Crystal Light. Blend well, and keep adding Crystal Light until you get your desired lip color. Wait several hours until the crystals dissolve, and then transfer to a small tin for use. And try to resist telling everyone what you've done when you get compliments on the shade!

—*Kelisa Pinto, via Facebook*

All-Natural Teeth Whitening Before you spend a small fortune on teeth whitening strips or procedures, try a banana instead. The inside of their peels contain both citric acid (a bleaching agent) and salicylic acid (an astringent that fights plaque). Rub one on your teeth after brushing for two minutes and they'll lighten stains naturally without harming your enamel.

Smooth-as-Honey Skin Treatment We love this all-natural remedy for skin blemishes—it's easy, effective, and cheap! Simply apply a drop of honey on top of the affected area and cover with a Band-Aid. Honey is loaded with healing enzymes that kill bacteria and toxins, reduce inflammation, and moisturize the skin. So the next time your skin acts up, just reach into your kitchen pantry for some sweet stuff.

Cellulite Solution If you're looking for a quick way to reduce the appearance of cellulite, try coffee! When rubbed against the skin, it helps to increase circulation and make the cellulite less noticeable. Here's our recipe for a cellulite treatment: In a small bowl, mix together ¼ cup ground coffee, 2 tablespoons sugar, 2 tablespoons honey, and enough olive oil until it's a damp paste. Massage over problem areas like your thighs, using a circular motion. Leave on throughout your shower, then rinse to reveal firmer-looking skin!

Soften Hands with a Sweet Scrub After all the yard work, crafting, cooking, washing, and general day-to-day living, our hands are often dry, cracked, and grungy—

especially in wintertime. To soften your rough skin, try this fresh-smelling exfoliating hand scrub, made entirely from ingredients found in your kitchen! Combine 2½ cups sugar, 1 cup olive oil, and 4 tablespoons lemon juice in a small mixing bowl. Stir until completely combined and the mixture is coarse and thick; then spoon into a jar or bottle with a lid.

Who Knew? Reader's Tip

Shower gel can get expensive, so make your own from the cheapest bar soap you can find. Use a cheese grater on two bars of soap, then add to 2½ cups warm water. Add a soothing oil of your choice (baby or almond oil work well), as well as rosewater or an essential oil like eucalyptus or marjoram. Refill an empty soap dispenser and shake. (You may need to shake each time you use it.)
—*Emma Louise Haydu, via Facebook*

Cuticle Cream Cost Cutter Did you know that cuticle cream contains almost the same ingredients as lip balm? Whether you did or not, you've probably noticed lip balm is much cheaper! Find a scent you like and apply directly to your cuticles to keep them healthy and prevent hangnails—at a fraction of the cost!

Delicious-Smelling Bath Salts Perfect for aches and pains, these vanilla-cinnamon bath salts smell like warm cookies once they hit the water! Mix together 1 cup Epsom salts, a teaspoon of cinnamon, and ¼ teaspoon vanilla extract, then pour into running bathwater.

Who Knew? Reader's Tip

If you love coconut-scented body butters, you'll love this all-natural homemade version. Head to an organic grocery store like Whole Foods and pick up a jar of pure coconut oil. Then hit up the essential oils section and pick any scent or scents you like. To make it, place some of the coconut oil in a bowl, and using a hand mixer, blend it until it's the consistency of whipped butter. Add a few drops of your favorite essential oil, and continue mixing until evenly combined. Transfer the mixture to a glass jar, and it's ready to use anytime your skin needs a little extra help. You'll be amazed how long the jar of coconut oil lasts, and how nourished your skin feels. —*Julie Norden, via Facebook*

Pampering Honey–Sea Salt Bath In this luxurious DIY bath soak, milk and salt provide gentle exfoliation, while the honey moisturizes. In a small saucepan over medium heat, heat 2 cups milk, ¾ cup honey, and ½ cup sea salt until dissolved. Cool slightly, and add this mixture to your bathwater, swirling to combine. You'll love the way it makes your skin feel and the way it smells.

DIY Foot Massage Make a foot soak even better than a foot massage with some marbles. Before dipping your feet in your favorite soaking solution (our favorite is a half a cup of Epsom salts and a two drops of essential oil), add a couple of handfuls of marbles to the bottom of the basin. Roll your feet over the marbles for an invigorating massage that increases circulation.

Homemade Hints for Healthy Hair

Just Add Salt Don't spend extra on a pricey shampoo that boasts sea salt as a volumizing ingredient—sea salt can be found in just about every grocery store! Just add a pinch to your regular shampoo and conditioner every time you wash your hair and you'll get the same volumizing effects.

Winter Wonder Hair Remedy Hate that winter scalp itchiness? This soothing egg and lemon shampoo will moisturize and soothe hair and scalp alike. Whisk two eggs together in a small bowl, then stir 2 teaspoons each of lemon juice, olive oil, and mayonnaise. Use in place of your regular shampoo, and condition as usual.

Who Knew? Reader's Tip

To keep your scalp naturally dandruff-free, use a little bit of lemon juice. Mix 2 tablespoons lemon juice with 2 cups warm water and pour over your head after you rinse out your conditioner. Let it dry in your hair and it will not only keep dandruff away, it will also make you smell wonderful.
—*Brandy Pastorino, via WhoKnewTips.com*

Homemade Volumizer If your hair is looking limp, try this unique trick. Soak ¼ cup rice overnight in a cup of warm water. In the morning, strain off the liquid into a spray bottle, and spritz it on damp hair. The starch will cling to each strand, creating lots of body and volume. And it barely cost pennies!

DIY Dry Shampoo Lately, we've noticed a booming new trend in hair-care products: dry shampoo. The idea is that this product can be used to revitalize less-than-fresh locks when you don't have time to wash your hair. But why spend anywhere from $3 to $15 on dry shampoo when you've already got the perfect substitute in your pantry? It's cornstarch. Granted, this tip is a little messy, so stand on a towel, or apply in the shower before turning on the water. Sprinkle a couple of tablespoons of cornstarch on dry hair and massage throughout the hair and scalp. Leave for five minutes to allow it to absorb excess oil, and then brush it out. Instantly revitalized hair!

Simply Smooth Conditioner This homemade conditioner will leave your hair smooth and manageable. In a bowl, whisk together two eggs. Then, stir in ½ cup water, 2 tablespoons olive oil, and 1 teaspoon apple cider vinegar, mixing thoroughly. Massage into clean, damp hair, and cover with plastic wrap or a shower cap. After 20–30 minutes, rinse thoroughly with warm water. Your hair will feel great, and you know every all-natural ingredient you put on it!

When Dye Needs to Die Uh-oh, you just tried dyeing your hair a new color, and it looks bad enough that you don't want to leave the house without a hat. What to do? Just wash it three or four times using an anti-dandruff shampoo that contains zinc pyrithione. This chemical diminishes dye more quickly without damaging your hair.

Savings Secrets for Beauty Products

The Best Part of Waking Up If you love the perfume section of the department store but sometimes get overwhelmed by all the scents, try out this trick: Just bring a cup of coffee with you! After you sniff one perfume, smell your coffee (or take a sip). You'll be able to smell the next scent fully, as if you just walked up to the perfume counter.

Man Up Did you know that on average, antiperspirants and deodorants made for men are $3 cheaper than their female counterparts—even when they have the same ingredients? If you're a woman who uses unscented deodorant, opt for the guys' stuff instead to save! You may also find a lightly scented variety you like.

Free Refills on Makeup Hooray for going green! Many cosmetics retailers now offer free products in return for bringing in empty makeup containers. M.A.C, for instance, will give you a free lipstick for returning six M.A.C. containers, while Lush will give you a free face mask for every five Lush containers you bring back empty. Kiehl's has a special card just for recycling Kiehl's containers, and has various rewards depending on the number of empty containers you return. Origins has to have our favorite recycling program, though. Bring in a container from *any* makeup (regardless of brand) and get a free Origins skin-care sample!

Who Knew? Reader's Tip

Most makeup is exactly the same, except for whether the manufacturer calls that shade of red you love "cherries jubilee" or "red crush." Make shopping for makeup easier by keeping an index card with your favorite colors on hand. Rub a bit of lipstick, blush, or eye shadow on the card, then mark down the brand and what the color is called. When it's time for more makeup, you can easily compare the colors of the sale brand with your card. Then write down what *that* color is called on your card. You'll soon have a list of all your favorite colors from each brand.

—*Arlene DeSantos, via email*

Strong Foundations Some of the most expensive makeup is foundation and powder. Make them last longer by buying a shade darker than your natural one, then mixing it with moisturizer (for foundation), or baby powder (for powder)

PLACES ONLINE
TO GET FREE COSMETICS

Test New Makeup Get free makeup as well as bonus gifts like a $50 Amazon.com gift card by joining PinkPanel, a company that connects beauty companies with product testers. To sign up, visit Facebook.com/thePinkPanel and click on "Join PinkPanel." Then like their Facebook page to get updates about beauty product testing opportunities!

Aveda Products If you like quality skin- and hair-care products, you'll love Aveda. Sign up for their email mailing list at Aveda.com, and you'll receive free samples and offers, like a free facial at one of their retail stores.

L'Oréal Luxury If you love L'Oréal makeup, you will be interested to know that they have a product tester program! Head to this super-secret address to fill out your information to apply to receive free L'Oréal makeup in exchange for your opinion: https://ConsumerTesting.LorealUSA.com/survey88.asp.

Alluring Freebies At Allure.com/freestuff, find makeup and other female-centric giveaways from *Allure* magazine. Though you aren't guaranteed the freebies you sign up for (you're entered into a contest), they have full-size samples and irresistible giveaways like 42 OPI nail polishes and free haircuts for life.

until it matches your normal color. You'll have more than twice as much, and you'll never be able to tell the difference!

Just a Dab Will Do You Do you find your perfume fading after a few hours? To make it last longer, rub a small amount of petroleum jelly onto your skin before you dab on your favorite scent.

Who Knew? Reader's Tip

When your mascara starts to clump, you don't have to toss it out! Smooth it out again by setting the tube in a teacup of near-boiling water for five minutes.   —*Deidre Fridolph, via Facebook*

No Ifs, Ands, or Butts Who knew diaper rash cream could help get rid of pimples? Dab a bit on offending areas, and the zinc oxide in the cream will dry up oil and kill bacteria, while the moisturizers will soften your skin. Meanwhile, it costs less than most store-bought acne treatments with the same ingredients.

Cheap Makeup Remover For an inexpensive way to remove mascara, eyeliner, and shadow, try baby shampoo.

It contains many of the same ingredients as eye makeup remover and works just as well, but costs a lot less. Pour a small amount on a tissue or cotton ball, rub over closed eyes, and rinse with water.

Super-Powered Deodorant To kick your deodorant's effectiveness up a notch, particularly on a very hot day, dust your armpit with baking soda after you've applied your usual brand. The baking soda will absorb excess moisture and fight odor.

Keep Razor Blades Good As New If your razor gets dull easily, it's probably due to rust that you can't even see. Keep rust away by storing your razor blade-down in a glass of olive oil. As a bonus, any olive oil left on the blades will help moisturize your skin!

Can the Cream Instead of buying expensive shaving creams or foams, try shaving with hair conditioner. (Buy the cheapest kind.) The conditioner will soften the hair and provide a layer of protection between your blade and your skin. You'll even get a closer shave!

Soothe Razor Burn Ouch! Your razor was a bit dull and now you have razor burn. Cure the redness and pain instantly by applying a layer of plain yogurt to the area. Let it sit for five minutes, then rinse off and pat dry. The lactic acid in the yogurt will calm your irritated skin.

Homemade Bubble Bath You don't need expensive bath gels to get a luxurious spa tub. To make your own bubble bath, use a vegetable peeler on a sturdy bar of soap, then place the slivers in a mesh drawstring bag. Attach the bag to the tap while the water is running. For even more fragrance, add in a couple of drops of favorite essential oil or herbs like rosemary and thyme.

DIY Bath Pillow To make your own bath pillow, reuse a household item no one seems to be able to get rid of: packing peanuts! Pour them into a large resealable freezer bag, then let out some of the air and seal. Place in the bath as a soft resting place for your head.

Golf Ball Massager You don't need to do a single thing to turn an ordinary golf ball into a massager for your feet or hands. Just roll it from the ball of your foot to your heel on the floor, or move in a circular motion between your two hands. It will even stimulate reflexology points that heal your whole body.

chapter 11

Lowering Your Bills

• •

Easy Ways to Save Electricity

Decreasing Your Heating and Air-
Conditioning Costs

Saving Money on Your
Water Bill

Your Cell Phone Bill, Slashed

Easy Ways to Save Electricity

Be a Night Owl You may not realize that most electric companies charge more for power during the day than at night. Contact your local utility to find out whether this is the case in your area. If it is, try to do all your laundry, dishwashing, internet surfing, and other power-intensive tasks during off-peak hours. We noticed the difference on our electric bill, and you will, too.

Take Them for Another Spin If you find your clothes are still dripping wet when you take them out of the washing machine, put them back in and set the cycle to spin. The extra spin time will wring them out even further, and use less energy than extra time in the dryer will.

Cut Drying Time Add a big, dry towel to the clothes dryer when drying jeans and other bulky items. It will cut the drying time significantly.

Save Your Cold Air A chest freezer will remain colder than an upright freezer when its door is open (even though its door is larger than an upright freezer's). This is because cold air is heavier than hot air and tends to stay

EASY REFRIGERATOR EFFICIENCY

Leaky Fridge? If your refrigerator is more than a few years old, the rubber lining that runs around the door (also known as the gasket) could be loose. To find out, close the door on a piece of paper. If you can pull it out without it ripping, your gasket is loose in that area. Try regluing your gasket or buying a new one from wherever you purchased your fridge.

Cool Runnings We'll admit it, this is a tough rule to stick to, but it's good to know! To keep your refrigerator running the most efficiently, don't overcrowd it. You want air to be able to move freely throughout the entire interior, so you should leave space next to each item.

Keep 'Em Closed Refrigerators use energy to reduce the humidity inside, which helps cool foods. Therefore, any time you leave an open container of liquid inside, you're wasting energy. Make sure all your pitchers have lids, and make sure dressings and moist leftovers are well covered.

Let Leftovers Cool Allow hot foods to cool before placing them in the refrigerator, so the fridge doesn't have to use extra energy to bring them down to room temperature. Of course, be careful with cooked meats, eggs, and poultry—they shouldn't stay out of the refrigerator for more than an hour.

put when the door of a chest freezer opens up. Meanwhile, an upright freezer releases most of its cold air the minute the door is opened. Buying a chest freezer can save you money both in energy costs and by giving you a place to store food you've made ahead of time, which will (hopefully) cause you to order in and eat out less. Check out Craigslist.org or eBay.com for people selling inexpensive secondhand freezers.

Ease Your Energy Bill Even when you're not using appliances, they still continue to use energy. So pull the plug when you're done with the blender, toaster, food processor, even your television—everything except appliances that need constant power to preserve a special setting.

Decreasing Your Heating and Air-Conditioning Costs

Keep 'Em Insulated Did you know that you could be losing warm (or cold) air through your electrical outlets? We placed some fireproof foam insulation under our outlet covers and switch plates and saved several dollars a month on our utility bill.

Get More Out of Your Radiator Brrr, it's cold in here! Wrap a very large piece of corrugated cardboard in aluminum foil (shiny side out), and place it behind your free-standing radiator. The foil will reflect the heat, and you won't have to keep telling your landlord to turn up the boiler.

Who Knew? Reader's Tip

Cut down on heating costs and keep your loved ones warm this winter by insulating your windows with bubble wrap. Yep, bubble wrap! The material is so inexpensive and easy to find, you'll be surprised at how well it works as insulation. All you'll need is the bubble wrap, scissors or a utility knife, and a spray bottle filled with water. First, cut the wrap to fit the size of your window. Spray a layer of water on the windowpane, and press the bubble wrap against it so the bubble-side is against the glass. The wrap will stick to your windows all winter long, just like that! If your bubble wrap needs extra adhesive help, use double-sided tape to keep it in place. *—Derek Bossert, via Facebook*

Easy Fix for a Stuck Thermostat If your furnace and AC don't seem to be paying attention to your thermostat, don't call the expensive repairman just yet. It could be a simple case of your thermostat's connectors being dirty. Take off the casing, and run the point of an index card through the connectors to remove any crud. Stand back and cross your fingers, and your thermostat may be as good as new.

Who Knew? Reader's Tip

If you have a sliding glass door that's rarely used during the winter, seal the top, bottom, and sides with duct tape to keep cold air from coming in.
—*Belinda Duchin, via letter*

Slow and Steady with the Heat When it's time to turn on the heat, be patient. Your house won't heat up any faster if you crank the thermostat way up, but you *are* likely to forget to turn it down, which can be a huge energy waster.

Keep It Humid It's true that it's not the heat that makes you feel warm, it's the humidity. Humid air feels warmer than dry air, so in the winter, instead of cranking the heat, run a humidifier. This allows you to turn down the heat, save energy, and still feel comfortable. Live, leafy plants also help raise humidity levels.

Close the Doors In the summer months, make sure to keep your closet doors closed. Otherwise, you're paying to cool your closets, which will increase your energy bill.

....

If You Were a Tree, Where Would You Be? One way we save money on our electric bill is by providing our house with natural shade. Planting trees and shrubs so that they shade the sunny side of your home will help cut down on the amount of air-conditioning needed. Just make sure not to plant trees too close to your home's foundation.

Saving Money on Your Water Bill

• •

Faucet Secret The easiest way to lower your water usage (and utility bill) is to screw low-flow aerators into your faucets. Aerators are easy to install, cost a dollar or less, and can save you $50 or more per year.

....

Hand Wash Separately Having an Energy Star dish-washer is energy-efficient, but not when you are running it twice a day. Cut back on the amount of space you take up in your dishwasher by washing large pots and pans the old-fashioned way—in the sink. By using a little extra water to wash these items separately, you'll save a lot of water in fewer loads washed.

Who Knew? Reader's Tip

Keep a spray bottle filled with water and a bit of dishwasher detergent near your dishwasher. If a dish is heavily soiled, spray it down before you put it inside. The detergent gets working on the food immediately, so you won't have to rinse your dishes before putting them inside, or run a separate "rinse" cycle before you do your dishes.

—*Elle Linden, via Facebook*

Skip the Dry Cycle Much of the energy your dishwasher uses is during the dry cycle, when it heats up water to the point of steam. To save energy, turn off the dry cycle (or simply open your dishwasher after the rinse cycle is done). Leave the door open a crack and let your dishes drip-dry. You'll save a lot by avoiding the heat-drying cycle on your machine, and your glasses will streak less.

Heat Less Water You never use your water on full-blast hot anyway, so it's worth it to lower how hot you keep your water heater. You can save up to $125 per year by simply lowering the thermostat on your hot water heater from 140° to 120° F.

Buy Your Water Heater a Jacket A water heater insulation jacket (also called a blanket) costs $15–$35, but it can cut the cost to heat your water dramatically. By insulating your water heater, you'll cut down on the amount of energy it needs to use to heat standing water in half, also cutting down on the amount you need to pay. To find out if you need a water heater jacket, touch the side of it. If it's warm, it's leaking energy.

A Pain in the Drain Make sure to drain your water heater once a year to get rid of sediment. Left too long, this grit can build up until you're using energy to heat sludge. To find out how to complete this simple home maintenance trick, type "how to drain a water heater" into Google or another search engine. And start to save!

Replace Those Showerheads! If the showerheads in your home were installed before 1994, you should seriously consider replacing them with their modern, energy-saving equivalents. Check out your local hardware store for low-flow alternatives, and remember that just because it's low-flow doesn't mean it has to be weak!

Wiser Washing The number one energy-sucker in everyone's home is usually heating hot water. Cut down on your bills by washing your clothes in cold water with a cold rinse. Due to advances in detergents and washing machines, the only time you really need to use warm or hot water is when you need to get a really bad stain, like red wine or oil, out of an article. Not only will you help the environment, you'll save money on heating the water, too.

Who Knew? Reader's Tip

If you have teenagers, try giving them an incentive to take shorter showers. A great one is five minutes added on to their curfew for every minute they shave off their showering time.

—*Salina Gonzalez, via email*

Leaky Toilets Mean Higher Water Bills Does your toilet have a leak? To find out, put a drop of food coloring in the tank and see if it shows up in the bowl. If it does, fix the leak to save up to 73,000 gallons of water per year!

Set It and Forget It If you've ever turned a sprinkler or soaker hose on and have forgotten about it, then the mechanical water timer is the gadget for you. Available at your local hardware store, these hose attachments work like egg timers and turn off the water supply after the amount of time you specify, usually between 10 minutes and two hours.

Your Cell Phone Bill, Slashed

How to Get Out of Your Contract Looking to change your cell phone plan but aren't sure how much you're going to have to pay to get out of your contract? Head over to CellTradeUSA.com, which will tell you how much it will cost to cancel. The site also allows you to transfer your contract to another CellTrade user, if your cell company allows it.

Are You Charged for Data Fees? If your cell phone company charges you data fees, make sure you only do high-data tasks while connected to a WiFi network. This includes streaming music and videos and downloading apps, music, podcasts, or any other content. Also keep an eye on any apps that may be using your location data in the background, as this will use up data. When surfing the web while on the go, mobile-optimized webpages will use less data than others, because they're stripped of the movies and advertisements that also make them load slowly. Finally, make sure your email on your phone is set to manually download, as your phone constantly checking for new emails can waste a lot of data minutes.

Who Knew? Reader's Tip

Ever wished you could create a ringtone of your favorite song? Well, www.IWFR.net/mp3toringtone makes it possible. Upload an MP3 file and the site will convert it to a file that your phone can use as a ringtone. —*Erin Corliss Giambuzzi, via Facebook*

Free Cell Plan You may have heard of the national "Lifeline Across America" phone program to help those who can't afford phone service. But did you know that this service is now available for cell phone plans? Qualifications vary by state, but for the most part, if you receive any kind of government assistance (other than Social Security) or make below a certain amount each year, you can get a free cell phone and 250 free minutes of talk time per month. You'll also receive free voicemail and text messaging! Just visit AssuranceWireless.com or SafelinkWireless .com to see if you qualify in your area.

Free Info Via Text Message Google isn't just for the internet anymore. Now if you need information on-the-go you can text Google with your cell phone. This is especially useful for addresses and phone numbers. Simply type in the business name and your city or zip code and text to 466-45 (G-O-O-G-L). Google will text you back with the information you need. You can even text "weather" and your zip code to get a three-day forecast. Normal text-messaging rates for your plan apply, but you won't be charged any extra.

App Savings FreeAppADay.com is our favorite site for free apps! They offer apps for iPhone, iPad, and Android that normally cost up to $4, but are being offered for a limited time for promotional purposes. Apps that are being offered change daily, so make sure to sign up for their email alerts or follow them on Facebook or Twitter!

Free and Easy Texts Did you know that just about every phone plan allows you to receive texts by email? To use your (or your friends') phone's email address, just type the phone number in the "to" field of your email and follow the @ sign with the following addresses: txt.att.net for AT&T customers, vtext.com for Verizon Wireless customers, tmomail.net for T-Mobile, messaging.sprintpcs.com for Sprint, message.alltel.com for Alltel, and vmobl.com for Virgin (for example, 2015551234@txt.att.net). Or get the phone's email address by sending yourself an email from it—just write a text message and enter your email address where you'd normally type the phone number. Just be aware that because your email address pops up, you can't always use the full 160 characters!

See Also . . . For tips on how to save money when you're buying a new cell phone, consult the chapter The Mall and Beyond: Savvy Shopping Tips

Saving on Internet, Home Phone, and Bundled Bills

Don't Forget the Taxes Did your bundled internet, cable, and phone company tell you that it's "cheaper to have a home phone number"? What they may not be telling you is that with taxes, having a home phone as part of your service may indeed cost you more per month. Make sure to ask the sales representative what the taxes will be, and if you do decide to go with the home phone, make sure it jibes with your first statement.

Take a Second Look Are you sure you know what's on your phone bill? Phone companies are notorious for automatically enrolling you in a calling package filled with services you never use. Make sure to check your phone bills for extra charges such as voicemail, three-way calling, and call forwarding. If you don't use these services, cancel them to save! If you use your cell phone more than your home phone, you might want to consider stripping your landline down to the bare minimum or canceling your service outright.

Who Knew? Reader's Tip

Yes, it may seem like a pain, but the best way to really make sure you're getting the best price on your bundled phone, internet, and cable plan is to call the company every six months or so and see if any discounts are available. Companies aren't required to notify you when new plans are available, so there may be a better plan for you that you don't even know about. Make sure to ask what taxes and fees will be included, and how long you will be "locked in" at that price. And enjoy the hold music!   *—James L., via WhoKnewTips.com*

Keeping Your Home Number Although households with no landline use an average of 332 more minutes per month on their cell phones than those with a landline, they still spend an average of $33 less per month on phone service. Consider going cell-phone-only in your household. If you don't like losing that phone number you've had for so many years, you should also know that the FCC mandates that phone companies allow you to "port" (transfer) your home phone number to a cell phone when you're first signing up for service with that company.

Calling Another Country When making international phone calls, never dial directly. Instead, buy an international phone card at your local convenience store. Most specialize in a particular country or continent, and will allow you to talk for only pennies a minute. You can also go to AITelephone.com, which works pretty much the same way, but gives you the option of prepaying online or receiving a bill.

Google Is Great Wish you could call someone right from your computer for free? Believe it or not, it's as easy as signing up for a Google account. Connect with your friends via IM and video chat, then click on "Call phone" to dial any phone number and connect instantly using your computer's microphone and speakers. Calls within the US are free, and they have better international rates than you will usually find with your phone company. For more information, visit Google.com/hangouts.

The Skype's the Limit Video chatting over the internet is a great alternative to using the phone. Our favorite service for free video chatting is Skype.com. It's easy to understand and easy to set up, and available online as well as on every type of tablet or smartphone. If old-fashioned phone-talking is more your pace, they also have voice chatting, with international rates that can't be beat. If you have an internet router with an extra plug, you can also plug your phone into it and use your phone instead of your computer! Calling other Skype members is free, and calls to other phones are only a cent or two per minute.

Use Other Companies to Your Advantage If you're lucky enough to live in an area that has more than one company providing phone, cable, or other utilities, use this to your advantage by lowering your payment amount—without having to switch companies! Find out what the competitors are charging by calling them or visiting WhiteFence.com, then call and ask for your rates to be lowered. If the first person you talk to says no, don't be discouraged and don't be afraid to ask to speak to a supervisor. If you call between 9 a.m. and 5 p.m. you'll be more likely to get an experienced supervisor on the phone who's willing to bargain.

Sharing Is Neighborly Do you and your neighbors both use wireless internet? A great way to save is to go in on an internet plan together. If you already have a plan, ask a neighbor you trust if they'd like to pay you for half the cost if you give them the password to your network. Especially if you live in an apartment building, you should be able to use the wireless internet hub you currently own, but if your homes are particularly far apart you may need to extend your network with a second hub or router.

Cheaper than Cable: TV Alternatives

Hulu Does It If you have a fast internet connection and a fairly new computer, you can watch TV and movies online for free! At Hulu.com, you can watch TV right on your monitor. Play the most recent episodes of shows from FOX, NBC, Comedy Central, and other networks; or classics like *The Dick Van Dyke Show* and *Alfred Hitchcock Presents*. They even have a good selection of movies, whether you're looking for something to entertain the kids or something R-rated for date night. Also, make sure to check out the websites of your favorite channels to see if they broadcast new episodes of their TV shows the day after they air on TV.

Free Online Movies At Crackle.com, you can find hundreds of free movies to watch online. They have an especially good collection of horror movies and comedy flicks, including lots of Monty Python. Also included are a few TV shows. You'll be surprised how many videos you'll find that are even more entertaining than an average night in front of the TV. Who needs cable?

More Video Options Though they're not free, there are several easy ways to watch TV and movies without paying for cable. At Netflix.com, you can get a monthly subscription to watch their large library of shows online, including many new favorites. If you have iTunes, you can download a wide variety of both TV and movies that are yours to keep. Amazon.com's "Prime" service also has free streaming videos, so if you're already paying for their free two-day shipping, make sure to check it out. They have several popular shows that aren't available on Netflix or iTunes.

Who Knew? Reader's Tip

You can save money by disconnecting your cable TV service during the times of year that you don't need it. Going on a long vacation? Have a summer ahead filled with time-consuming activities? Just get rid of the cable during the time you won't be using it, and who knows, you might even be offered an enticing deal when it's time to re-subscribe.
—*Brandon "B-Rock" Johnson, via Facebook*

Stream Your Video! With cable bills soaring, you probably know more and more people who have opted to get rid of their cable service. The good news is, it's easier than ever before to enjoy online entertainment right on your TV. For the cost of just one or two cable bills, you can invest in a streaming video unit like Roku or Apple TV, which allows you to select Netflix, Hulu, and other programming right from your remote (certain video game systems, like Xbox and Playstation, also allow you to do this). If you already have a BluRay player, this service is probably built in. A new and inexpensive option is Google's ChromeCast, but an even more inexpensive option is simply buying the right cord to hook up your TV to your computer! Consult your user's manual, or Google the make and model of your computer and/or TV. You may need to buy more than one cord and hook them together, but if you have a newer TV there is usually an option to hook it up as a second monitor. If your computer doesn't automatically pump the sound through to your TV, simply use your computer's headphone jack to hook it up to some speakers.

The Library: More than Just Books Obviously, libraries are full of books you can borrow for free. But did you know that many libraries also carry DVDs? If there is a particular movie or TV show you are looking for and it's not available at your local branch, ask a librarian to get it for you through inter-library loan. Libraries are also a great place to get magazines. If you don't mind reading back issues, save on subscriptions by getting older copies at the library. This is especially great for kids' magazines (because kids won't know the difference!). You never know what items your library might have in circulation—many offer musical instruments and more—so make sure to ask a librarian.

Sports Without Cable These days, you can cut your cable and practically not notice, thanks to all of the TV shows and movies available on streaming services. But if you're a sports fan, you'll be hard hit—watching *Breaking Bad* five years after the episode aired is one thing, but watching your favorite team win the pennant is something completely different! Fortunately, there are a few options for watching live sports that are still cheaper than shelling out for that ultimate sports package your cable provider wants you to buy. First, look into getting a TV antenna. It may be old-school, but if you get good reception you'll still be able to keep up with your team. Your next options are the streaming services of the various pro sports organizations—the NFL, NBA, and NHL, as well as Major League Baseball all have streaming "season passes" that you can buy to watch games on your computer or mobile device. The bad news is that most of these plans cost more than $100, but they also allow you to watch every game played, not just games in your market. It's a godsend for sports fans who don't live in the same area as their teams!

Saving Money on Insurance, Bank Fees, and Miscellaneous Expenses

Time to Drop Collision Coverage? When your auto insurance renewal comes in the mail, don't just write a check and send it in. Review your policy and make sure it's still the type of coverage you need as your vehicle ages year after year. When it gets to the point where your collision coverage premiums (plus the deductible) are almost the same as the value of the car itself, drop that portion of the coverage—you're only flushing money down the toilet.

Security Pays Did you know that most homeowners' insurance policies will deduct 3–5 percent of your cost for adding simple security features such as a smoke alarm or dead bolts? You can often save a lot more if you're willing to install a more sophisticated security system. These systems can get expensive, but the savings (not to mention the security) may be worth it. Before you choose one, make sure to call your insurance company to see what kind of system they recommend. You may also to be able to save if you are 65 or over.

Improvements Pay Off A big factor in how much you're charged for homeowners insurance is where you live. So if there have been improvements to your neighborhood or subdivision, such as storm drains being installed or a fire hazard being cleared away, make sure to alert your insurance company and see if they will lower your rates.

Walk into Savings If you need medical treatment but can't afford a doctor, consider a walk-in clinic. Walk-in retail clinics can be found in many drug and even department stores. You'll see a nurse or nurse practitioner and may get everything you need, with the convenience of the pharmacy on-site. Besides the quick service and low cost, you'll appreciate the extended evening and weekend hours. Remember these clinics are meant for minor illnesses and injuries such as colds and flus, sprained muscles, pinkeye, burns, and ear infections. If your situation goes beyond the scope of the clinic, you'll be advised to see a doctor.

Who Knew? Reader's Tip

If you have healthy teeth and gums, you may not need dental insurance. Check the rates of your premium, because you could be paying more in insurance than you would if you simply paid the dentist out-of-pocket for your regular cleanings and X-rays.
—*Lynnette Feagin Gebhardt, via Facebook*

Free Cleanings for Kids Did you know that the first Friday in February each year is Give Kids a Smile Day? Dentists around the country provide free checkups and cleanings to kids on this day, so if you schedule your kids' 6-month checkups in February and August, that's one less cleaning you have to pay for! Visit the American Dental Association's website at GiveKidsASmile.ADA.org for more information.

TAX SECRETS

Job Search Write-Offs Save those receipts when hunting for a new job in the same line of work you're currently in. Many of your expenses may be tax deductible—phone calls, photocopies, traveling to interviews, career counseling, and more—even if you do not get a new job.

Medical Deductions If you itemize your deductions on your yearly tax return, you can deduct medical and dental expenses for you and your family (if an elderly parent is your dependent, this can really add up!). The bad news is that you can only deduct the amount of these expenses that exceeds 7.5 percent of your adjusted gross income (AGI). To learn more, see IRS Publication 502: Medical and Dental Expenses.

For the Gamblers If you happen to find yourself in the lucky position of having net gambling winnings near the end of the year, maybe it's a good time to treat yourself to a gambling vacation. Net winnings are taxable (and can only be offset by gambling losses), but net loses are deductible. So if you lose on your trip, you'll be able to write it off. And if you happen to win on vacation, well just consider it your lucky year.

Do the Smart Thing Getting a refund? Resist the urge to spend the refund and fill out the box to get it put into US bonds instead. These bonds are a great investment because you don't have to pay any federal income taxes on the interest earned on them until you cash them in.

Beware the Gas Card Take an extra-careful look at credit cards offered by gas companies—most have a higher interest rate than average credit cards. Before you sign up, make sure to ask about their fraud protection, which is usually pretty weak. You may be better off using a "regular" credit card that offers rebates on gas purchases. Two good choices are the Discover Open Road card and the Chase Freedom card.

Who Knew? Reader's Tip

Credit card interest is calculated based on your average daily balance over the month, which means you can reduce your charges by making more payments. Instead of paying, say, $300 at the end of the month, split that up into two $150 payments. That way, your average daily balance will be lower, and therefore your finance charges will be, too.

—Craig Masterson, via WhoKnewTips.com

Why We Love Credit Unions Tired of all the fees and high interest rates at your bank? Consider joining a credit union instead. CUs are not-for-profit, member-owned institutions, thus allowing them to be more beneficial for every account holder—not just the ultra-wealthy ones. We've also found that, if you need a loan, they are more open to talking with you about what you need it for and how you plan on paying it off, instead of just looking at the numbers and denying you. To find one in your area and determine if it's right for you, visit NCUA.gov and select use thier Credit union locator.

Save the Date Here's an easy solution if you keep getting socked with late fees, or neglect to pay more than the minimum on your credit cards because the payment is always due at the same time as your rent. Ask your credit card company to change the date your payment is due. It might take a few months to kick in, but you'll be able to pay down the card more easily during the part of the month that isn't as much of a crunch.

Balance Transfers If you owe lots of money to one credit card and not as much to one with a lower interest rate, ask your credit card company if you can do a balance transfer. You may incur a fee, but you often end up saving in the end, and many cards offer them for free during the first year of your agreement. If you have two cards from the same company, ask if the card with the better deal allows "credit reallocation," which would let you transfer not only the balance from the other card but its credit limit as well, without even submitting you for another credit check.

Index

Owho knew?
online

Visit us at
WhoKnewTips.com!

* New tips every day
* Who Knew? books and ebooks
* Videos, freebies, and much more!

Add us for the
Who Knew? Tip of the Day!

@WhoKnewTips